Ghosts In The Bedroom

A Guide For Partners Of Incest Survivors

By Ken Graber, M.A.

Health Communications, Inc.
Deerfield Beach, Florida

Credit:
"The Stages" from *THE COURAGE TO HEAL* by Ellen Bass and Laura Davis. Copyright
©1988 by Ellen Bass and Laura Davis. Reprinted by permission of Harper Collins
Publishers.

Library of Congress Cataloging-in-Publication Data

Graber, Ken. Ghosts In The Bedroom: a guide for partners of incest
survivors / by Ken Graber.
    p.   cm.
Includes bibliographical references.
ISBN 1-55874-116-X
    1. Incest victims — Psychology. 2. Incest victims — Family rela-
tionships. 3. Adult child sexual abuse victims — Psychology.
4. Adult child sexual abuse victims — Family relationships.
    I. Title.
IHQ71.G73 1991   90-4878
362.7'6—dc20   CIP

©1991 Ken Graber
ISBN 1-55874-116-X

Publisher: Health Communications, Inc.
                 3201 S.W. 15th Street
                 Deerfield Beach, Florida 33442-8190

D E D I C A T I O N

This book is dedicated to Patty,
my wife and life partner,
whose love and support have been
a courageous and precious gift.
Whatever I know about relationships
has been learned through our commitment
to solve life's problems together.

ACKNOWLEDGMENTS

To Dr. Sidney Simon and Suzanne Simon, whose Values Clarification Strategies and Values Realization Workshops inspired me to take action for my own personal recovery, and from whose example I found the courage to risk sharing of myself in person and in writing.

To Dr. Wayne Murphy and Michael Tarpinian who encouraged me to start this project and who had no doubt that I could write this book.

To Dr. Jacqueline Carroll, Mary Fraker, Mary Gosney, Martha F. Graber, Suzanne Simon and Sandra Wara de Baca who reviewed the draft manuscript and provided invaluable comments and suggestions.

To my children, Cybill Graber Morton, Seth Torbert and Tara Torbert Wenning, who have encouraged me and whose growth has challenged me as a parent.

To all the incest and sexual abuse survivors and their partners whose experiences and sharing have taught me many lessons in recovery.

To Robert Saunders whose artistic talent is evident in the back cover photograph.

To Health Communications, Inc., and my editors, Kathleen Fox, Lisa Moro and Marie Stilkind, who have made publication of this book possible.

CONTENTS

INTRODUCTION

My name is Ken Graber and I am the partner of an incest survivor.

I first learned that my wife was an incest victim within our first year of living together. She described the incident in vague terms with little emotion and seemed reluctant to say more. This was a secret between her and her father, the abuser. No one else in the family knew about it. I listened and comforted her but did not ask her to go on. I did not know what to say and was afraid to get into it any deeper. My wife did not seem to be suffering at that time from any significant effects of the incest experience other than a deep distrust for her father.

Many years later, after the death of her father, my wife began to feel the effects of the incest experience. She began to be depressed and cried easily. Our sex life began to suffer. At first she discounted the possibility that these feelings had anything to do with her childhood experience because she had only been fondled. She believed that for the experience to be damaging, the abuse must have been more flagrant or the experience more violent. However, the feelings did not disappear, and she realized they deserved to be taken seriously. She started individual therapy with a therapist knowledgeable about recovery from incest and a short time later joined a survivor support group. Today she is well on her way toward recovery.

I also recognized that my personality defects had contributed to our relationship problems and began attending a support group to deal with my own co-dependency. What I learned in that group helped me to support my wife's recovery without getting entangled in her issues. I am a voracious reader and I scoured the literature to find guidance for partners of incest survivors. I have read almost all the books on incest and sexual abuse, and with the exception of a few brief chapters and paragraphs, I found nothing helpful.

In talking about my experience with others, I found that
this is a common problem for partners of sexual abuse survivors. To provide mutual support and begin to remedy this
situation, I helped organize a support group for partners of
survivors. This has given us a place to talk about our experiences and share our feelings with others who are similarly
situated. This group is open to partners of either sex and any
sexual orientation. We have found that, in spite of obvious
differences among us, our experiences and feelings are more
similar than different.

1

Am I The Partner Of A Survivor?

If you are the partner of a sexual abuse survivor, you are not alone. Recent studies show that by the age of 18 one woman in three and one man in four has been sexually molested. It has been estimated that these statistics are low due to under-reporting, especially for male victims. It is also known that these statistics are based on a definition of sexual molestation including only the most flagrant kinds of overt childhood sexual abuse.

Self-declared sexual abuse survivors also include those who were forced to hear or see others abused, exposed to pornography, involved in voyeurism or exhibitionism, verbally abused and raped or abused as adults. When the definition of sexual abuse is broadened to include these additional kinds of overt and covert sexual abuse, both child and adult, the number of survivors and the number of partners of survivors are significantly increased.

There has recently been a large increase in the literature available for sexual abuse survivors and the resources needed to assist their recovery. Survivor support groups are also springing up in many communities. Although there are nearly as

1

many partners as there are survivors, and although partners
are significantly affected by the survivor's recovery process,
there is almost no literature and little support for partners.

It is a confusing time for both partner and survivor when
the survivor's memories begin to return. It is appropriate for
the survivor who experienced the primary trauma to be in
treatment, but the partner often has nowhere to turn. Partners
cannot turn to survivors for support because the survivors are
too busy with their own issues and it would be inappropriate
for them to divert energy away from their recovery.

Some of the feelings that are natural for partners would be
hurtful if expressed to the survivor. But suppressing their
feelings is not healthy for partners either. Partners need their
own support network so they can get healthy or stay healthy
and be supportive of the survivor's recovery. Although friends
may be willing to listen or offer support, they may not be
helpful unless they also have knowledge of the issues for
survivors and partners of survivors. The best solution is for
partners to have their own program and their own group.

The largest group of survivors are females who are in relationships with male partners and who were abused by males.
However sexual abuse survivors can be of either sex and any
sexual orientation. So can their partners. Male partners may
be in heterosexual relationships with female survivors or gay
relationships with male survivors. Female partners may be in
heterosexual relationships with male survivors or lesbian relationships with female survivors.

Regardless of these apparent differences, the commonality
of experience and feelings for partners in all circumstances
predominates. The commonality for partners also spans the
type of sexual abuse. All partners can find comfort and understanding whether the abuse was heterosexual or homosexual,
whether there was incest, sexual abuse or rape, and no matter
what age the abuse occurred or the current age of the survivor.

What Is Sexual Abuse?

Sexual abuse is the term used to refer to any incident that
causes an individual to feel sex-related shame. It includes

sexual molestation or abuse, incest and rape. These terms are used in an expansive sense that includes subtle and isolated incidents as well as flagrant and continuing experiences. They apply to victims of either sex. Incest is between family members and the victim is usually a child under the age of 18. Sexual molestation or abuse also involves a child victim but is not between members of the same family. Rape involves force or violence and may be directed against a victim of any age.

Sometimes the definition of incest is extended to include sexual abuse by any person in a position of authority or responsibility. This definition is compatible with the sense of betrayal and violation of trust experienced by incest survivors. It makes little difference whether a survivor's abusive experience meets some particular definition — the recovery process is the same. Partners of sexual abuse survivors are even further removed from the experience and need only understand its damaging effects whatever the duration or type of abuse.

Physical molestation includes flagrant and easily recognized acts of sexual abuse. Some of the most common are oral sex performed by either party, vaginal or anal intercourse and vaginal or anal penetration with fingers or objects. Physical acts of sexual molestation also include manual sexual contact or stimulation and masturbation by either individual. In some cases children are induced to have sexual contact with animals. A little less obvious is fondling or sexualized touching of other areas of the body and inappropriate sexual kissing and hugging.

Children need to be touched, cuddled, kissed and hugged in nurturing and appropriate ways. In healthy families there is a clear distinction between appropriate and inappropriate touching. Dysfunctional families with confused, unclear boundaries allow touching to be inappropriately sexualized, which children experience as sexual molestation. Other physical acts that can become sexual molestation are excessive and stimulating tickling, erotic or bare-bottom spanking, intrusive or unnecessary enemas and excessive personal involvement in toilet training.

In addition to physical acts, there are kinds of sexual abuse that do not involve contact. Voyeurism and exhibitionism are

examples. Peering through windows or displaying explicit
pornography are clearly voyeuristic, but less obvious is looking
through open doors and refusing to respect a family member's
privacy in dressing, bathing or using the toilet. Exhibitionism
is the counterpart to voyeurism and occurs in many of the
same situations. Healthy adults take care to model privacy and
protect children from the sight of adult nudity and sounds of
adult sexual activity.

Verbal sexual abuse is a final type that can also have shaming and damaging impact on the child. Obscene telephone
calls can be frightening and shaming, particularly when found
in conjunction with an excessively prudish family that refuses
to allow age-appropriate sex education or discussion about
anything sexual. The opposite extreme of a family that allows
young children to be exposed to crude sexual jokes, inaccurate
sexual information or too much sexual knowledge too soon
can be equally damaging. Sexual abuse also includes sexual
threats, graphic descriptions and other inappropriate sex talk.

The key elements characteristic of sexual abuse are lowered
self-esteem and imposed shame. Sexual abuse does not occur
where there is respect for the individual's identity, boundaries
and self-esteem. When these are violated the victim — who
had less power in the first place — feels responsible for the
violation, loses self-esteem and takes on the shame.

What Does "Survivor" Mean?

Survivors are persons who were victims of sexual abuse. In
some ways "victim" and "survivor" are interchangeable, but
there is a difference in focus. The term "victim" is most frequently used in the courts and legal settings where the focus
is on the incident or crime. The term "survivor" is used in
counseling and self-help programs where the focus is on the
individual's treatment and long-term recovery. In the early
stages of recovery the survivor feels like a victim. Using the
term "victim" may inhibit further recovery. Consciously holding up the image of "survivor" assists those stuck in the
victim role to see recovery as a possibility.

It is also helpful for partners of sexual abuse survivors to use the term "survivor" since recovery is a process that affects both the survivor and the partner. Using the term "survivor" keeps the focus on the person who has been abused and their responsibility to actively seek and take part in their recovery. The term "survivor" gives credit to the effort the person put forth in order to survive the ordeal, recognizing that some victims did not survive. Identifying oneself or one's partner as a survivor is a hopeful designation that reinforces belief in the possibility of growth, change, recovery and regaining full functionality and health.

How Do Survivors Recover?

Recovery for survivors of sexual abuse is usually a process that takes from three to five years of therapy and participation in a support group for survivors. The period of time required for healing and recovery depends on how deeply damaging the sexual abuse experiences were, but the three- to five-year guideline fits in almost all cases.

Sometimes the healing period appears to take longer because the survivor takes time out to deal with other issues, and sometimes it appears to be shorter because the survivor has previously dealt with part of the abuse issues. Some survivors spend a few months working on the sexual abuse issues and gain some measure of recovery but leave some deeper issues unresolved. These may be dealt with at a later time. There is no set schedule for recovery. Each individual proceeds through the various stages at their own pace.

In their book *The Courage To Heal*, Ellen Bass and Laura Davis have described the stages of survivor recovery they have observed:

The Stages

Although most of these stages are necessary for every survivor, a few of them — the emergency stage, remembering the abuse, confronting your family, and forgiveness — are not applicable for every woman.

The Decision to Heal

Once you recognize the effects of sexual abuse in your life, you need to make an active commitment to heal. Deep healing happens only when you choose it and are willing to change yourself.

The Emergency Stage

Beginning to deal with memories and suppressed feelings can throw your life into utter turmoil. Remember, this is only a stage. It won't last forever.

Remembering

Many survivors suppress all memories of what happened to them as children. Those who do not forget the actual incidents often forget how it felt at the time. Remembering is the process of getting back both memory and feeling.

Believing It Happened

Survivors often doubt their own perceptions. Coming to believe that the abuse really happened, and that it really hurt you, is a vital part of the healing process.

Breaking Silence

Most adult survivors kept the abuse a secret in childhood. Telling another human being about what happened to you is a powerful healing force that can dispel the shame of being a victim.

Understanding That It Wasn't Your Fault

Children usually believe the abuse is their fault. Adult survivors must place the blame where it belongs — directly on the shoulders of the abusers.

Making Contact With The Child Within

Many survivors have lost touch with their own vulnerability. Getting in touch with the child within can help you feel compassion for yourself, more anger at your abuser, and greater intimacy with others.

Trusting Yourself

The best guide for healing is your own inner voice. Learning to trust your own perceptions, feelings and intuition forms a new basis for action in the world.

Grieving And Mourning

As children being abused, and later as adults struggling to survive, most survivors haven't felt their losses. Grieving is a way to honor your pain, let go and move into the present.

Anger — The Backbone Of Healing

Anger is a powerful and liberating force. Whether you need to get in touch with it or have always had plenty to spare, directing your rage directly at your abuser, and at those who didn't protect you, is pivotal to healing.

Disclosures And Confrontations

Directly confronting your abuser and/or your family is not for every survivor, but it can be a dramatic, cleansing tool.

Forgiveness?

Forgiveness of the abuser is not an essential part of the healing process, although it tends to be the one most recommended. The only essential forgiveness is for yourself.

Spirituality

Having a sense of power greater than yourself can be a real asset in the healing process. Spirituality is a uniquely personal experience. You might find it through traditional religion, meditation, nature, or your support group.

Resolution And Moving On

As you move through these stages again and again, you will reach a point of integration. Your feelings and perspectives will stabilize. You will come to terms with your abuser and other family members. While you won't erase your history, you will make deep and lasting changes in your life. Having gained awareness, compassion, and power through healing, you will have the opportunity to work toward a better world.

Partners of survivors are involved in every stage of recovery and can be a strong source of support if they understand the survivor's recovery process. A common pattern is for the survivor's memories to begin returning sometime after the age of 30. By then the survivor is trying to establish a mature sense of identity and feels safely removed from the influence of the abuser. Some survivors may begin recovery earlier, while some may not feel safe enough to deal with the issues until after the death of their abuser.

Am I The Partner Of
A Sexual Abuse Survivor?

Questionnaire A

	Yes	No
1. I am the partner of someone who has a lot of hangups about sex or about reasonable sexual variations.	——	——
2. I am the partner of someone who doesn't seem to be involved when we have sex.	——	——
3. I am the partner of someone who usually wants or needs drugs or alcohol in order to have sex.	——	——
4. I am the partner of someone who has a strong negative reaction when touched in a certain way.	——	——
5. I am the partner of someone over 30 who has begun having disturbing sexual memories or dreams about childhood.	——	——
6. I am the partner of someone who I think may have been the victim of incest, sexual abuse or rape.	——	——
7. I am the partner of someone who thinks they may have been the victim of incest, sexual abuse or rape.	——	——
8. I am the partner of someone who was the victim of incest, sexual abuse or rape.	——	——
9. I am the partner of someone who is in a recovery group or is in therapy for victims of incest, sexual abuse or rape.	——	——

If you answered YES to any of these nine statements, you are almost certainly the partner of a sexual abuse survivor.

Questionnaire B

	Yes	No
1. Was my partner raised in an alcoholic or other dysfunctional family?	—	—
2. Is my partner in the Alcoholics Anonymous, Al-Anon or Adult Children of Alcoholics recovery program?	—	—
3. Does my partner have an eating disorder such as overeating, anorexia or bulimia?	—	—
4. Is my partner moody or someone who cries easily and frequently or suffers from prolonged depression?	—	—
5. Does my partner frequently space out or lose track of a conversation for no apparent reason?	—	—
6. Is my partner often accident-prone during unremembered time periods?	—	—
7. Is my partner afraid to have children? Or children of a particular sex?	—	—
8. Is my partner very uneasy about being around adults of a particular sex?	—	—
9. Does my partner frequently wear inappropriately tight or revealing clothing?	—	—
10. Does my partner frequently wear loose clothing or excessive layers of clothing?	—	—
11. Does my partner compulsively have sex or love relationships?	—	—
12. Does my partner almost exclusively use sex to get money, control or affection?	—	—
13. Does my partner have siblings who were victims of incest or sexual abuse?	—	—
14. Has my partner engaged in self-mutilation, self-tattooing or threatened suicide?	—	—

If you answered *YES* to three or more of these 14 questions, you are very likely the partner of a sexual abuse survivor.

2

It's Driving
Me Crazy

Indirectly the partners of sexual abuse survivors are also victims of sexual abuse. Partners include lovers, spouses, intimate friends, family members or anyone who is in a relationship with a survivor and is affected by the survivor's feelings and actions.

The survivor is usually not fully aware at first of how extensive the impact of the sexual abuse experience is, and in many cases does not even remember that it occurred. The experience of sexual abuse is so powerful and devastating that survivors are rarely able to describe it to their partners, and the partners are understandably perplexed. Sexual abuse casts a shadow of confusion over survivors, partners and their relationships.

The partner senses there is something wrong in the relationship that seems to have no explanation. Sexual relationships often lack feelings of intimacy and joy and sexual relations become either infrequent or desperately driven. The sexual abuse survivor remains moody and depressed in spite of the partner's persistent attempts to be supportive and cheerful. The partner sees that the survivor is in pain and may be driven into apparently irrational actions. Out of love for the survivor and empathy with the survivor's feelings, the partner is affected by the sexual abuse.

If you are a partner of a sexual abuse survivor and feel you have been affected by the survivor's experience, you may be feeling confused, frustrated, angry or a variety of other feelings. It is good to know you are not alone and that many other partners have these same feelings. The feelings and reactions described in this chapter are based on partners' sharing of common experiences during the early stages of the survivors' recovery.

> **Note:** All individuals described in this book are composites of many sexual abuse survivors and partners. There are no direct quotations of anyone but the author. Any similarity of the examples to any specific person is the result of our common characteristics.

As you follow the descriptions you may note similarities with your own situation and feelings. You may relate to some and not others. Gather what comfort you can from these sharings and remember these are temporary feelings that you will resolve in your own recovery. Your healing is your own responsibility and is not necessarily tied to the survivor's recovery.

I Can't Figure Out What's Wrong

A very high proportion of sexual abuse survivors deny the existence, the duration, the severity or the effects of the experience. This denial is often a self-preservation technique that is essential for survival to adulthood. Even when survivors can recall the incest, sexual abuse or rape, they often are in denial about its ongoing effects. They may be saying, "I've already dealt with that and put it behind me. I don't need to talk about it anymore." If the survivor doesn't know or acknowledge what's wrong, the partner is even more confused.

I know something is wrong, but I can't figure out what it is. Connie says it's nothing and that she doesn't know why she feels weepy and depressed. I think she trusts me and would tell me what's going on with her if she knew what it was. I don't know if it's something I said or did or what. I feel like I'm going crazy.

Let me back up a minute. Connie is very emotional and she cries over every little thing — songs on the radio, touching TV commercials, sad movies, happy movies, weddings, you name it. She's also got PMS pretty bad and gets irrational and depressed. But this isn't her time of the month and everything in our life is going great. I just don't understand.

This is how one partner described the situation just before the survivor recovered her memories. As long as denial is operating about sexual abuse or its effects, it looms as an unseen specter that drags down the survivor and partner alike.

I Suspected It

As the survivor begins to open up about the sexual abuse and its effects, many times it comes as no real surprise to the partner. Instead it feels like finding the missing piece of a jigsaw puzzle.

I could tell she had some kind of serious hangup about sex from the way she sometimes pulled back when I touched her. I wasn't being rough or anything; I must have just touched her in the wrong spot. I even asked her once if she had been sexually molested, but she said, "No." I guess she wasn't in touch with it or wasn't ready to deal with it then, but I think on some level both of us knew about it for a long time.

For most survivors, awareness and disclosure are continuing and incremental processes during the early stages of recovery from sexual abuse. Rarely does full recall of the abuse experiences, the feelings and their effects occur all at once. The memories of the sexual abuse experience may not initially be available or may not be complete. They return as the survivor is ready to deal with them. As partial memories emerge some survivors remember the event first without the feelings, some remember feelings not clearly associated with any event and some remember neither event nor feelings but see the effects in their bodies or behavior.

A sensitive partner may be the first to notice the behavior, see the effects in the body or hear the feelings and recognize the possible connection to prior sexual abuse. In this case, the partner can gently help the survivor come to the same realization. Unless the relationship between partner and survivor has deteriorated, the partner will be a part of the survivor's growing recognition of the sexual abuse and its effects. Together they can acknowledge what both somehow knew but couldn't express.

I Can't Believe It

Partners are also subject to deep denial. At first some partners are unable to accept the disclosure as factual. This reaction is more common in the unsuspecting partner who is stunned at the revelation. With no background for any other response, the partner may fall into denial as a protection against the common social attitude of repugnance and disgrace that surrounds sexual abuse.

> I couldn't believe it. I just couldn't believe it. I know her dad, and he's a nice guy. There's no way it could have happened like she said. It's got to be some kind of fantasy. It couldn't have happened if she just told him not to.

It's unfortunate when the partner has this response, especially if the partner expresses these feelings to the survivor. This is one of the times when it is better for partners to work out their feelings with their own support network. It's tough enough for the survivor to break through denial and reveal the shameful memories of sexual abuse without also having to break down their partner's denial.

The partner's denial may be perceived as an accusation of the survivor and may temporarily inhibit further recollection or disclosure. It may be helpful for both partners and survivors to acknowledge the statistics that show the prevalence of sexual abuse and to give full credit to the survivor's emerging awareness. If there's any hint of sexual abuse experiences having occurred, they probably did.

I Didn't Bargain For This

Partners have a right to be angry. Anger is a natural and healthy response to being hurt, and partners are also hurt by the sexual abuse. Even against the partner's intentions, the first expression of anger may come out as blaming or wanting to escape from the reality of the situation.

> Before this happened, we were doing okay. We loved each other, our relationship was great, the kids were doing fine, my career was beginning to take off. There were no problems. Now everything's shot to hell. We aren't getting along, the kids are acting up and I can't get my work done.
> I didn't bargain for any of this when we got together, and now I just want to get out. It feels like I got set up to take a fall, and it's not my damn fault.

Many partners have these feelings, and it's not wrong or bad to feel this way. But it is hard for the survivor, who may already be having overwhelming abandonment issues, to hear feelings like this expressed. Here again it is better for the partner to work out these feelings with other friends in the partner's own support network.

It's true that the partner did not ask for it, but neither did the survivor. Both partner and survivor are victims and neither one deserves the pain and suffering. Blaming resolves nothing. It's better to accept the reality of the situation, take responsibility for its betterment and channel the energy of the anger into recovery and positive change.

This Is The Nth Time

Sometimes a partner finds out that this is number "N" in a series of relationships with sexual abuse survivors. Given the statistics, it's not surprising for this to happen once or twice. But if it's an ongoing pattern there's probably a reason that should be examined.

> "Oh no, not again" was my first thought when Gwen told me she thought her father had molested her when she was nine. I've been through this with three other women and Gwen is my fourth incest victim in a row. I didn't even see it coming, and I ought to know what to look for because it happened in my family. I'm beginning to think there's something about me that attracts them. I thought she was so healthy, but "Wham!" It hit me again.

Relationships begin with a selection process in which two people are attracted to each other and feel comfortable with each other based on common experiences and compatible levels of functioning. Sexual abuse survivors not in recovery model their behavior on the dysfunctional relationships they observed and learned as children. They often project a certain kind of need. Partners who were raised in dysfunctional families themselves may respond to this and feel comfortable in a relationship where they can act out the same roles they used or observed in their family of origin.

This often results in people repeatedly selecting similar types when initiating relationships. It is common to gravitate toward a person who resembles the parent who was least nurturing or the parent with whom there is the most unfinished business. How many of us are still trying on some level to please Mommy or Daddy?

Our Relationship Is Deteriorating

Partners with no knowledge about the recovery process for survivors often have a lot of uncertainty about changes in the relationship. As the survivor moves into recovery and begins changing, the relationship is affected. These changes continue throughout the three- to five-year recovery period, and partners who are unprepared for the changes may think the relationship is being destroyed. In fact, recovery makes more fulfilling intimate relationships possible, but the relationship may seem to get worse before it gets better.

The relationship problems begin almost immediately and often continue throughout recovery. At first as the survivor's memories begin to emerge, there may be periods of moodiness, crying spells or depression. Later as the survivor identifies sexual abuse as the problem, the relationship may become secondary to the survivor's preoccupation with the issues of sexual abuse. Problems with sexuality, a topic worthy of consideration on its own, may pervade the relationship. Intimacy in the relationship is also affected by commitment and trust. Before the sexual abuse issues are finally resolved, the partner may feel the survivor is using recovery issues to take over all control in the relationship. Descriptions of how these problems come up may help partners understand that they are common ones.

Recognition of sexual abuse as a major life issue happens gradually as the survivor sees its effects in more and more areas of life. The universal characteristics are low self-esteem and shame coupled with other symptoms such as sexual dysfunction, dissociation, poor body image, painful body memories, flashbacks, prolonged sadness or depression and moodiness or crying spells.

> I don't know what's wrong. She's become so depressed she doesn't want to go to work, take care of the kids or do any part of the shopping or housework. On weekends she won't get out of bed and get dressed unless we have to go somewhere. I'm doing just about everything that gets done, and I can't keep up with it.

If the relationship lasts long enough for the issue of sexual abuse to be identified, the partner may think problems will soon be resolved. Instead, the survivor becomes increasingly aware and concerned about the effects of sexual abuse. As more and more of the survivor's energy goes into thinking about sexual abuse, reading about sexual abuse and talking about sexual abuse, the partner may begin thinking the relationship is not worth saving.

> She became obsessed with it. She literally told everyone that she was an incest victim. She took any break in the conversation as an excuse to bring it up. When she wasn't talking about incest, she was buying and reading every book in the bookstore. I couldn't get her to pay any attention to me or anything else that was going on.
>
> And if that wasn't enough, she just let herself go. She wasn't eating right or taking care of her clothes. She kept getting into one of those moods when she would hurt herself or threaten suicide.

Partners need to know this is one of the stages in recovery. It may be mild and brief or severe and prolonged, but it too shall pass. There is hope for better things to come.

Problems such as these test the degree of commitment in the relationship. Even if the relationship is able to weather these early problems, others will come up during the course of recovery. For survivors, trust and abandonment are two of the core issues that must be resolved. Survivors' early experiences and memories cause them to be fearful of placing trust in anyone and constantly wary of betrayal and abandonment. When a partner's overtures are met with distrust and suspicion, the partner's natural tendency to withdraw triggers the survivor's feelings of abandonment. This reinforces the validity of the survivor's feelings and deepens the spiral of distrust and betrayal.

Survivors are also suspicious of anyone who exerts any degree of power and control over them. Healthy relationships have an equitable division of power and control that is flexible and remains in balance as it changes to meet changing circumstances. In contrast, partners and survivors must struggle continuously to maintain a balance and avoid misunderstandings over the ebb and flow. It sometimes seems that the partner has to give up too much to avoid offending the survivor.

When do my wants and needs get taken into account? It feels like I'm always the one who defers. Sometimes I'd like to pick the restaurant and movie. You know what I'd like? I'd like to get physical without worrying about being careful. What if I'm turned on and want to make love?

Relationship problems aren't easy, and they occur throughout the recovery process. But awareness is one of the keys to success. If partners understand that these problems are common and expected — and that there is hope — then there is a good chance the problems can be resolved. In later stages of recovery the relationship can reach higher levels of intimacy than ever before.

Sex Life? What Sex Life?

Most partners know there are problems with sex in the relationship or sense that sexual intimacy is not all it could be. It makes sense that the survivor's sexuality would be affected since sexual abuse caused the underlying problem. But partners may not be aware of or understand how many ways that survivors' sexuality can be affected.

Of the many problems with sexuality, partners most often complain about the survivor's lack of sexual desire and reluctance to have sex. A healthy partner naturally desires to include sex among the ways to express loving intimacy in the relationship. It's difficult to understand why the survivor is not receptive to this. It's even harder for many partners to accept the moratorium on sex that most survivors need at some stage during the recovery process.

I've always thought of sex as a kind of barometer that gives a reading on the health of the relationship. If the sex is good and intimate, the relationship is doing okay. If sex is strained and doesn't feel right, the relationship is in trouble.

When we got together, sex was great and we were close together. Then it got so she hardly ever wanted to do it and I didn't want to force her. It wasn't that she refused, it was just that she seemed to avoid being available for sex. At night she would either already be asleep when I got to bed or she would stay up so late that I would fall asleep. In the morning she would either get up and be dressed before me or stay asleep until I lost patience and got up myself.

When we talk about it, she always says she loves me, she's physically aroused by me and she wants to make love, but it just doesn't happen very often. It's usually good for both of us when we do make love, but it's over pretty quick because I'm so sex-starved that I don't last very long. I'm a better lover when we make love more often.

Last night she dropped a bombshell on me. She said that while she was working on her incest issues we couldn't have sex. She didn't just say it like that; we actually talked about it for a long time. But it still blew me away. Of course I agreed. I'm not a rapist and I don't want her to do it if she doesn't want to.

She talked it over with her counselor and they agree that it's what she needs right now for her recovery. She said she doesn't want to be unfair to me but this is something she has to do for herself. She doesn't know how long it will be, and she's working hard on her issues because she doesn't want it to be any longer than necessary either. I'm trying to be understanding, but I feel like part of me has just been put on ice for the duration.

At the other extreme, some partners are faced with survivors who press for almost constant sexual attention. Survivors who were induced to attach their self-esteem to their sexual attractiveness and ability to please are driven to act seductively and seek sex frequently. The survivor may sexualize every interaction, regardless of the partner's wishes or intentions.

At first I liked it; it was like a honeymoon. We made love every day, sometime two or three times. She could sure turn me on. She knew where every one of my buttons was and loved pressing them, and I loved to have them pressed. We never fought; we were too busy having sex.

Then it started to get a little irritating. When I tried to be serious and refused to respond, she'd pout until I took her to bed . . . again.

These survivors too must place a freeze on sex until recovery enables them to regain a healthy sense of self-esteem and place sexuality in its proper perspective. In such cases, the partner may almost find it a relief.

Many partners complain of unfulfilling sex. The survivor is not responsive and is not fully present during sex. Male survivors may have difficulty sustaining an erection, and female survivors may be nonorgasmic. No matter what stimulation or technique is used, the partner and survivor don't seem to be connecting. This lack of real intimacy and contact at the body level is almost universal when the sexual relationship between partner and survivor is a problem.

Am I Doing It Wrong?

"Is there something wrong with me?" is what many partners wonder when all self-help efforts fail to improve their sexual relationship. It is common for partners to begin to call themselves into question and suffer a loss of self-esteem from internalizing the problem. Partners may be bewildered by the survivor's seeming lethargy or diminished responsiveness.

> Brenda was always kind of subdued when we made love. But one time when I started to go down, her breathing got real shallow and she wasn't moving at all — she'd fallen asleep. "What the hell's going on?" I wondered. "I may not be a dynamic lover, but I'm not that bad."

Partners need to learn not to take it personally when they are affected by a survivor's abnormal sexual behavior. Although the partner is involved, the survivor's behavior is primarily determined by the survivor's history of sexual abuse and the resulting internal feelings and thought processes.

I Can't Take The Acting Out

Many partners have problems dealing with survivors who act out in various distressing ways. Examples of acting-out behavior include promiscuity or prostitution, self-mutilation, and crisis-producing behavior. Caring partners worry when they see this kind of self-destructive behavior and try to talk the survivor out of it, hoping to bring the survivor back into control.

> Why is she cutting herself? I don't get it. She's already in so much inner pain and turmoil, why would she want to hurt some more? I've told her a hundred times that I love her and care about her and to call me first at any hour of the day or night. It's crazy for her to keep doing it, and it's getting to me too.

The survivor's acting-out behavior in some strange way gives the survivor a way to dominate the disturbing memories and exert a little power and control over the aftermath of sexual abuse. The partner cannot control the survivor's behavior. Probably, neither can the survivor. Attempts to stop the acting out are likely to be ineffective until the survivor's underlying sexual abuse issues are identified and addressed.

Why Am I In So Much Pain?

A partner who loves and cares about the survivor is naturally going to feel sympathy for the survivor. In many cases, however, the partner's feelings go beyond healthy sympathy. The partner empathetically identifies with the survivor and internalizes the survivor's pain.

> She's such a sensitive and sweet person and she's in such overwhelming pain. Whenever we are together the tears just come. I am overcome with sadness. I feel like I'm struggling to stay afloat, and she may be going down for the third time. She's such a beautiful woman and I love her so much . . .

When the partner's pain begins to approach the same level as the survivor's, the partner has a problem of co-dependency and over-identification. The key is detachment with love.

Detachment is finding clarity about which issues must be faced by the partner, which by the partner and survivor together and which by the survivor alone. Detaching with love means being an ally. It is supporting the survivor in facing personal issues without trying to take over or direct the survivor's recovery and without taking on or taking offense at the survivor's expression of emotion. There is a distinction between a healthy partner providing sympathetic support and an unhealthy partner taking on the survivor's problems.

I'm Not The Enemy

When survivors begin ceasing self-blame and appropriately placing blame on the one responsible for the abuse, they may place a blanket condemnation on all individuals who are the same sex as the abuser or have any superficial resemblance to the abuser. In this stage, any attempt by the partner to initiate sex or even to initiate nonsexual contact may trigger rejection and accusations.

> When I get the least bit romantic or approach her in any way, she pushes me away and says, "You men are all alike" or "Would you *please* get away from me and leave me alone." I know she's not rejecting me personally and that she's trying to work through her feelings toward her father because she's told me so. But it still hurts when it happens and I'm afraid we'll never be intimate again.
>
> If I can just let the words go by without getting caught up in the emotion, I can say, "I'm not your father. I'm not going to hurt you. You are safe with me." If I stay calm and deflect the anger toward her father, sometimes it turns the situation around.

This is one of the ways that things seem to get worse during the survivor's recovery, but actually it is a sign of getting better. The survivor is beginning to develop a sense of identity separate from the experience of abuse and is beginning to separate the present from the past. At first the separation is incomplete. The partner is confused or lumped together with the abuser and all external reminders of the experience. By recognizing this as progress and supporting the completion of the separation, the partner can validate and facilitate the survivor's growing sense of identity.

I'm Full Of Rage

After getting over the initial denial, many partners are angry about the sexual abuse. The first feelings of anger are often not focused at anyone or may even be misdirected at the survivor. As the reality of the events and their effects become clearer, the anger becomes more consistently directed toward the abuser where it belongs.

> I get furious whenever I think about what he did. She was an innocent child who did not deserve to be treated that way and she has a right to be angry. It hurts me too, and I have the right to my anger too. I feel like I could kill him or worse. I'm going to make sure he never gets to her again.

Hold on to your anger and rage. It's the source of the energy you will need to complete the recovery and healing process. Do not be too quick to dismiss the anger with a statement like, "I know he was a victim too, and he didn't mean to do it. He was just doing the best he could with what he had at the time." *If you can't get angry, you can't get well.*

Anger is intended to let us know when we have been threatened or hurt and give us the energy to protect ourselves and resolve the problem. Anger used properly helps us take appropriate action to stop or counteract the threat or hurt and to channel the energy into constructive problem resolution. Use this energy to pursue your own recovery as the partner of a sexual abuse survivor.

READER/CUSTOMER CARE SURVEY

If you are enjoying this book, please help us serve you better and meet your changing needs by taking a few minutes to complete this survey. Please fold it & drop it in the mail. **As a thank you, we will send you a gift.**

Name: _____

Address: _____

_____

Tel. # _____

(1) Gender: 1) _____ Female 2) _____ Male

(2) Age: 1)____ 18-25   4)____ 46-55
2)____ 26-35   5)____ 56-65
3)____ 36-45   6)____ 65+

(3) Marital status:

1)____ Married 3)____ Single 5)____ Widowed
2)____ Divorced 4)____ Partner

(4) Is this book: 1)____ Purchased for self?
2)____ Purchased for others?
3)____ Received as gift?

(5) How did you find out about this book?

1)____ Catalog   2)____ Store Display
Newspaper
3)____ Best Seller List
4)____ Article/Book Review
5)____ Advertisement
Magazine
6)____ Feature Article
7)____ Book Review
8)____ Advertisement
9)____ Word of Mouth
A)____ T.V./Talk Show (Specify) _____
B)____ Radio/Talk Show (Specify) _____
C)____ Professional Referral _____
D)____ Other (Specify) _____

(6) What subject areas do you enjoy reading most? (Rank in order of enjoyment)

1)____ Women's Issues/   5)____ New Age/
Relationships   Altern. Healing
2)____ Business Self Help 6)____ Aging
3)____ Soul/Spirituality/ 7)____ Parenting
Inspiration   8)____ Diet/Nutrition/
4)____ Recovery   Exercise/Health

(14) What do you look for when choosing a personal growth book?

(Rank in order of importance)
1)____ Subject   3)____ Author
2)____ Title   4)____ Price
Cover Design   5)____ In Store Location

(19) When do you buy books?

(Rank in order of importance)
1)____ Christmas
2)____ Valentine's Day
3)____ Birthday
4)____ Mother's Day
5)____ Other (Specify _____

(23) Where do you buy your books?

(Rank in order of frequency of purchases)
1)____ Bookstore   6)____ Gift Store
2)____ Price Club   7)____ Book Club
3)____ Department Store   8)____ Mail Order
4)____ Supermarket/   9)____ T.V. Shopping
Drug Store   A)____ Airport
5)____ Health Food Store

Which book are you currently reading? _____

Additional comments you would like to make to help us serve you better.

_____

_____

Thank You !!

FOLD HERE

BUSINESS REPLY MAIL
FIRST CLASS MAIL PERMIT NO 45 DEERFIELD BEACH, FL

POSTAGE WILL BE PAID BY ADDRESSEE

HEALTH COMMUNICATIONS
3201 SW 15TH STREET
DEERFIELD BEACH, FL 33442-9875

NO POSTAGE
NECESSARY
IF MAILED
IN THE
UNITED STATES

3

My Core
Issues

In forming relationships we seek partners who are at our
same level. For example, co-dependents repeatedly establish
relationships with drug addicts or alcoholics. When we meet
people who are at our own level there is an immediate rapport
and sense of comfort. We very quickly feel that we belong
together. This occurs before either person has said anything
about alcoholism, drug addiction, co-dependency, dysfunctional families or sexual abuse. We know how to find each
other and we feel most at ease with someone whose behavior
is familiar, someone who dances the same dance.

Finding ourselves in a relationship with the survivor of
sexual abuse means we must look at ourselves to see why we
were attracted to a person like that. Even if the sexual abuse
issue had not been identified when we met, at a subconscious
level we were in tune with each other and were communicat-
ing on the same wavelength. If we are in a close personal
relationship with a sexual abuse survivor who is active in or
needs therapy or a recovery program, it follows that we also
need therapy or a recovery program.

This is an essential rule. If one partner in a relationship needs or is receiving treatment, the other partner is also in need of treatment. Both may be in need of treatment as a couple or family. Generally speaking, both must move to resolve their own core issues at the individual level before relationship issues can be addressed. If one partner in a relationship receives treatment and moves into recovery and the other partner does not, it is very unlikely that the relationship can be sustained for long.

Thinking that all would be well and wonderful except for the survivor's problem is a form of denial. So is agreeing to participate in a few therapy sessions to "find out what's wrong with the survivor." Remember that we are unconsciously attracted to others who remind us of our family of origin. If we recognize any dysfunction in the survivor, it is highly likely that we are also the products of a dysfunctional family and have problems of our own. Similarly, recognizing that survivors come from dysfunctional backgrounds probably means that they were attracted by some of the same dysfunctions in us.

Recovery works best, not when the survivor is identified as the problem that needs fixing, but when both partner and survivor are committed to personal growth and working on their own issues. Common issues and relationship issues can be worked on together. If as partners we refuse to face our own problems and fail to work toward correcting our behavior and eliminating dysfunction in the relationship, then the survivor in recovery will be the one who outgrows us and leaves. It enhances the program of both partner and survivor if we can walk through recovery as equals.

If we wish to remain in a relationship with a survivor of sexual abuse, it is imperative that we look within ourselves, identify our own core issues and take responsibility for our own recovery. Core issues are problem areas where there are repeating patterns of behavior that are destructive or that limit us from attaining our full potential. Recovery literature includes various lists of core issues and volumes of material for dealing with each one. There are also numerous self-help groups and 12-Step recovery programs that address one or more of the core issues.

Categories Of Core Issues

There are four categories of core issues that we must consider in our self-examination: primary dependency, secondary dependency, co-dependency and shame-based identity. Although there are some overlapping among them, these categories are useful in figuring out where to start. The core issues in each category are described to guide us in our self-examinations and are presented in the order they should be considered.

Primary Dependency

Primary dependency includes alcoholism and other drug addictions. These addictions are characterized by an uncontrollable urge to experience the effects of the alcohol or drugs. They are considered primary due to the extensive nature of the associated mental and behavioral distortions. Left untreated, they progress rapidly toward institutionalization and death.

Alcoholism and drug addiction are primary, progressive and potentially fatal diseases. Primary means that active alcoholism or drug addiction must be treated first and brought under control before underlying family, social or psychological factors and other core issues can be addressed. Progressive means that these diseases can only get worse; their development can be arrested by abstinence but they can never be cured. Potentially fatal means that these diseases can and do kill.

Primary dependency is its own core issue that over-rides all others. It is not possible to effectively deal with any other core issue if a primary dependency is active. We cannot recover from anything else if we are not first straight and sober. Resources for primary dependency include Alcoholics Anonymous (AA), Narcotics Anonymous and various outpatient and inpatient treatment programs.

Secondary Dependencies

Although they may also be very serious, secondary dependencies are usually not as immediately life-threatening and usually do not cause over-riding mental and behavioral distortions. Their effects range from mild to severe and they should be considered in light of the magnitude of their impact on our lives. Some of the common secondary dependencies are eating disorders, overworking, compulsive shopping, gambling and smoking, all of which have their own recovery programs and resources. The central core issue of the secondary dependencies is avoiding feelings by the diversion of the compulsive or obsessive activity.

In our dysfunctional families we did not learn to express emotions in functional ways. Our parents were uncomfortable with their feelings and could not model healthy emotional behavior. Most of us grew up with the family rules, "Don't talk, don't trust, don't feel." If feelings were expressed at all, they appeared in outbursts of emotion that were often directed against the children. Feelings were something to be feared and suppressed. As a result of our upbringing, we learned to stuff our feelings and use compulsive or addictive behavior to keep them down.

In most cases, a severe secondary dependency inhibits our ability to fully feel the emotions associated with other core issues. This means it is difficult or impossible to begin work on other issues while our secondary dependencies are out of control. We do not have to be fully recovered from secondary dependencies before turning our attention to other issues, but it is helpful if they are at least brought under control. We may continue to be active in a secondary recovery program at the same time we begin dealing with our deeper core issues.

Co-dependency

Co-dependency has also been defined many times in recovery literature and usually includes a list of core issues such as boundary deficiency, detachment, over-control, people-pleasing and caretaking. Co-dependency is characterized by a focus on the feelings, wants and needs of others that prevents us from effectively dealing with our own. Left untreated, co-dependency is also a fatal disease associated with death due to cancer, hypertension and heart disease.

Co-dependents turn all our attention to the concerns of others, largely ignoring our own emotional needs for fear of being thought selfish. As a result we are lonely and emotionally empty. We give enormous amounts of compassion to others and never receive any. We have many friends but few intimate, nourishing relationships. We are steady and reliable workers, willing to go to any length to meet the needs of others and then dismiss compliments with, "It was nothing." Yet everything we do is designed to gain the approval of others. We overcommit ourselves and are afraid to say "no" for fear of encountering disapproval. We are afraid to get angry, turning our anger inward where it is converted into depression. We can only assert ourselves as protectors of the disadvantaged and have great difficulty asking for anything for ourselves.

As partners of sexual abuse survivors, we often find our co-dependency issues brought up through our involvement with the survivor and the depth of pain and feeling elicited by the sexual abuse issues. Even if we have resolved co-dependency issues in other situations, our intense personal involvement with the survivor is likely to trigger it again. Support groups for partners specifically addresses co-dependency in this context.

It is a common myth or misconception that co-dependency is bad for the co-dependent but good for the object of the attention. In fact it is bad for both. Co-dependents cannot become healthy because their energy and attention are directed away from self-discovery and away from taking responsibility for their own lives and issues. The co-dependent's well-intentioned activity also interferes with the recovery and health of the dependent or object of attention. This occurs because the dependents are prevented from fully experiencing the natural consequences of their actions and do not learn to take responsibility for their own recovery.

Our personal recovery depends on our recovery from co-dependency. The resources available for co-dependents include Al-Anon, Co-dependents Anonymous (CODA) and various self-help groups, particularly those dedicated to personal recovery for supporters of people with special problems, illnesses or needs.

Shame-Based Identity

Shame-based identity involves a continuous state of self-consciousness about something within that is dishonorable, improper, disgraceful or unworthy. It is a despairing sense of identity based on these inner feelings. It is marked by the feeling of being unworthy at the very core of one's being. Shame-based identity includes all the core issues associated with low self-esteem, growing up in an alcoholic or dysfunctional family, physical abuse, incest, sexual abuse or other types of abuse. This category also includes core issues related to self-limiting or self-destructive behavior such as low achievement, self-sabotage, delinquency, anti-social behavior, sex and love addiction and various types of neurosis, psychosis and mental disorders.

Shame is the painful feeling arising from the consciousness of something dishonorable, improper, disgraceful or unworthy done by oneself or another. Guilt and embarrassment are similar but less painful feelings of being caught or exposed doing something we know is wrong. Shame is a deeply painful feeling of personal inadequacy.

Members of healthy families normally experience some degree of guilt or shame as they learn the boundaries of acceptable behavior. The feeling of shame is resolved by open discussion and positive change before the shame becomes internalized. In dysfunctional families, repeated patterns of shaming, distrust, miscommunication and painful interaction cause the almost constant feelings of self-shame and family shame to become internalized. When internalized, this continual shame becomes the basis for a despairing sense of identity based on inner feelings of defectiveness or deficiency, feelings of being unworthy at the core of one's being.

Living with a shame-based identity is more than most of us can take without finding something to numb the ever-present and painful feelings of inadequacy. Addictions and compulsive behavior are the most frequent mechanisms we use to alleviate our inner discomfort and feelings of shame. Regardless of the source of shame, the result is almost always an addiction or a compulsive behavior disorder. The addictive and compulsive behavior is an attempt to find an external solution for core issues caused by a shame-based identity.

Characteristically, shame-based identity core issues are more about ourselves than they are about anyone else. Even if someone else contributed to their cause or is involved in their manifestation, we feel the effects primarily within ourselves and we are responsible for dealing with the issues. Even when we are in denial about these core issues, we usually have a sense that the problem is inside us. When we are ready to face the issue, we are looking in the right direction.

The Adult Children of Alcoholics (ACoA) program is directly relevant for most of these core issues. Other resources include Sex and Love Addicts Anonymous (SLAA) and Incest Survivors Anonymous (ISA) as well as other specific issue-oriented groups. Individual or group therapy and different kinds of support groups are also clearly a part of an overall treatment approach for these issues.

As partners of sexual abuse survivors, we should pay particularly close attention to the possibility that we are sexual abuse or incest survivors ourselves. Remembering that we are often drawn to others who are on our same level and have similar issues, this is worth giving some second thought to. Is it possible that we are in denial about this issue in ourselves? Do we have an exaggerated interest or fascination with the survivor's personal issues that may indicate we have the same ones?

If any one of the four categories seems relevant, you should identify the core issues that apply, locate the resources for that category and begin your recovery there. Although there are variations depending on the degree of severity, recovery from any of the major core issues is a process that usually takes from three to five years. If this sounds like a short time, it is because we have been struggling with the issue for a large part of our lives, unsuccessfully using the wrong resources. If this seems like a long time, look on it as a promise of recovery. The sooner you begin, the sooner you will start to feel better. In starting a recovery program, there is often an initial period of confusion when the feelings and issues seem overwhelming. But if we stick it out and keep coming back, we will find ways to deal with the feelings and issues one at a time. In pursuing the path of recovery, we find hope for better times full of happiness and joy.

4

Supporting
The Survivor

When someone we love has been hurt, it's natural for us to
feel compassion and want to nurture and offer comfort. Since
we also experience the hurt empathetically, it's also natural
for us to feel anger and want retaliation. We are involved and
we want to be helpful, but we don't know what to do.

The combined experience of partners and sexual abuse
survivors who have recovered indicates that partners can be
helpful in supporting the survivor. Again, the first and most
helpful thing partners can do is to become healthy and mature
functioning adults themselves. The partner's function in supporting the survivor is a job for someone who is healthy or
progressing in recovery. A healthy and functional partner can
speed the survivor toward recovery, while a dysfunctional
partner in denial impedes progress. To be helpful the partner
needs to develop some support skills to use in relationship
with the survivor. These skills are like the ones needed for any
successful relationship, but a special sensitivity is needed that
goes beyond what may be otherwise required. As the survivor
progresses in recovery, there are specific tasks that often in-

volve the partner. A supportive partner can be aware of these tasks and may be instrumental in their successful completion.

The Partner's Function

In supporting the survivor, the partner must guard against co-dependent behavior. As partners we are responsible for our own recovery only, not the recovery of the survivor. It is not our role to try to exert undue influence or control over another's life. We can, however, stand behind the survivor to offer appropriate support and validation for the survivor's recovery.

Co-dependent behavior is characterized by focusing on someone else's interests to the detriment or exclusion of one's own. Healthy and independent behavior is characterized by a primary focus on oneself and a secondary focus on others. This means that we remain in balance and retain a healthy and independent sense of ourselves as we offer appropriate support in interaction with those we love. Healthy independence is like holding hands, while co-dependency is like chaining heart and soul.

Reality Mirror

As human beings we need to have some idea how we appear through another person's eyes. In infancy and childhood this is often fulfilled by seeing ourselves in the mirror of our parents' eyes. The loving eyes of healthy parents enable us to see ourselves as wonderful, special and worthwhile individuals, while the distressed eyes of dysfunctional parents create feelings of shame and worthlessness. Sexual abuse survivors need to re-experience the process of seeing themselves through the mirror of loving eyes to reclaim their sense of self.

Partners need only look with open and loving eyes on the survivor and honestly express the reality they see. If the partner sees the survivor as unique and lovable, then the survivor can begin to give up the internal image of being a damaged, shameful and worthless person. In the process of recovery the survivor's self-esteem and self-image often lag behind the external reality. In mirroring reality by looks, words and touch, the partner can help the survivor bring internal and external perceptions together.

Dysfunctional Co-dependence	Healthy Identity
My good feelings about who I am stem from being liked by you.	I like myself and who I am without being affected by others.
My self-esteem depends on my receiving your approval.	I give myself approval and generate my own self-esteem.
My serenity is seriously affected by your problems.	My serenity is based on solving my own problems.
I focus on solving your problems and relieving your pain.	I focus on solving my own problems and my own pain.
My attention is centered on trying to please you or protect you.	I do what gives me pleasure as long as it is not hurtful to others.
I try to figure out ways to manipulate you in order to help you.	I can only change myself and offer you the benefit of my experience.
My self-image is affected by your good or bad behavior.	My self-image is based on how I act and feel myself.
I feel boring without you and put myself and my interests aside to take up yours.	I am an interesting person and I enjoy sharing and exchanging interests with others.
I give up taking care of myself in order to take care of you.	I practice good self-care and don't expect others to take on my duties.
How I feel about myself depends on how good you look.	I feel good about myself and the way I look.
I can only feel good when I know you are feeling good.	I am in touch with my own feelings, whatever they are.
I don't want anything for myself; I only want what you need.	I know my own wants and take care of my own needs.
I will do anything to avoid being rejected by you.	I know I am a worthwhile person.
I let you have your way because I am afraid of your anger.	Conflict is a part of life and I resolve differences constructively.
I can't make a decision without getting your opinion.	I know my own mind and make healthy personal decisions.

Example Of Health

Individuals in close personal relationships often pick up traits and characteristics from each other. By associating with those who are healthy or who have achieved a measure of recovery, we can observe functional behavior as a pattern for our own behavior. Since partners are sometimes less damaged than survivors, partners who are serious about recovery may progress faster than their mates. A partner who is further along in recovery can serve as an example of healthy behavior.

This works best when it is done in a spirit of humility. It is a gift to be capable of setting the example of healthy and functional behavior. This need not be a burden; in fact it happens naturally. Just doing our best is all it takes for our behavior to rub off on others and for them to adopt a higher level of functioning. Recovering adults begin to be able to recognize healthy, functional behavior and can choose to adopt new models to replace or supplement defective parental models. Recovery means redefining a sense of identity to conform with healthy models and reforming a sense of belonging by attaching to a functional support system.

No one can be perfect or is expected to be. Acknowledging weaknesses and promptly admitting mistakes is part of modeling healthy behavior. Partners and survivors can help validate each other's healthy and functional behavior by saying: "I liked it when you did . . ." or "I'd like to be able to act like you did when . . ."

Confidant

Sexual abuse survivors are often burdened with the stated or unstated demand to keep the abuse a secret. Dissociation, repression, suppression, shame and occluded memory are also barriers that keep recollection of the abuse buried. Since we are only as sick as our secrets, it is important to facilitate disclosure by being a confidant and listening to the survivor.

In being a confidant to a sexual abuse survivor, the first and most important guideline is to *believe them*. Even if some of the facts seem wrong or improbable, the feelings are absolutely true. The survivor has taken a great risk by sharing memories and feelings about the sexual abuse experience and deserves to be believed. Parts of the story may be missing, the circumstances cloudy or the persons involved only partially identifiable, but the story is as accurate as the survivor can remember or express. Believe the story first. Greater detail and accuracy may come out as the survivor progresses in recovery.

The second important guideline for the confidant is to *accept what you hear without judgment*. It takes great courage for a survivor to disclose the sexual abuse experience and to trust you with the painful and confused feelings associated with the memory. Accepting the story with nonjudgmental understanding is necessary for the full story to come out. Ask if there is more to tell or if the survivor would like to elaborate on some of the details, but don't press for what the survivor is not ready to tell. Don't say anything about the experience that the survivor might internalize as disapproval or a moral judgment. Confidants can show survivors that they are not rejected for revealing their secret fears, their deepest hurts, and their worst mistakes. Listening without judgment is a message that they are still accepted even after telling their most shameful secrets, the ones they were afraid to admit to another human being.

Even if the story or parts of the story have been told before, let the survivor tell it again and again until there is nothing left to say and the emotional content of the experience has been resolved. It is by telling the story that the survivor can begin to make the experience real and deal with the feelings that surround the experience. Feelings that the survivor must express are likely to resurface during the telling of the story, and the survivor may need to stop and process the feelings before proceeding further with the story. Let the survivor come to their own understanding of the experience, their feelings and their meaning.

Trusted Friend

Partners need to be trusted friends for survivors. It is difficult for survivors to develop trust, since sexually abusive experiences can damage the ability to trust at a very basic level. A trusted friend affirms the reality of the survivor's experience, saying: "I see the sadness in your tears. I hear the loneliness in your voice. I sense the pain in your body. I perceive the abandonment in your eyes. I understand the betrayal of your experience." Being a trusted friend means saying: "I will be there for you when you hurt. If you want company, I'll be with you. If you want to be alone, I understand. When you want to talk, I can hear anything you need to say."

Giving the survivor permission to express emotions honestly without fear of consequences, no matter what the emotions, can be the beginning of trust. After a feeling of trust has been established, additional details and more personal emotions will follow. By telling highly personal details, survivors have exposed their vulnerability. The partner needs to show that the trust has not been misplaced and that the survivor's vulnerability is safe. A trusted friend will respect boundaries and will not commit physical, mental, emotional or spiritual violations. It is particularly important to avoid sexual violation when dealing with recovery from sexual abuse.

In the process of talking about the sexual abuse experience, recovering the memories and processing the feelings, there may be sexually explicit discussions. Such discussions are for the purposes of recovery and are not to be interpreted as a lowering of the sexual boundary or an invitation for sexual activity. In fact, it is usually advisable to avoid sexual activity for a period of time after a discussion about the sexual abuse, so the survivor can process any feelings or realizations that have come up without confusion. In some cases partners may be asked to support sexual abstinence during the survivor's recovery.

The trusted friend or partner in recovery can support the survivor by acting as an ally, advocate or sponsor. This means encouraging change without manipulation or pressure, listening without directing. It means not trying to do it ourselves or taking over. The support comes through when we avoid unnecessary criticism and give affirmations in abundance.

Skills To Develop And Use

Developing and using good relationship skills can enhance the quality of any relationship and is particularly important for the partner of a sexual abuse survivor. Perhaps the most important skills are good communication, dialogue and problem-solving skills. Without honest and open communication to provide the basis for identifying and resolving differences, the relationship has little chance for success. Another set of skills are those needed to remain engaged in the work of building the relationship. These include attention to relationship issues from moment to moment, combined with a commitment to stick with it through difficult times and the flexibility to try various solutions.

Differences of opinion and even anger are not necessarily signs that the relationship is in trouble. In fact anger can be used to strengthen the relationship if we develop the skill of using it constructively. We can learn to avoid turning the anger against each other and to treat each other with the utmost gentleness and sensitivity. To maintain a successful relationship with a survivor of sexual abuse, a special delicacy is needed that takes into account the sensitizing effects of the abuse experience. Since sexuality is a highly charged issue for survivors, we must use our sensitivity to avoid irritating contact and place greater emphasis on nonsexual intimacy. Our level of intimacy can actually increase even through a moratorium on sexual activity.

Strong relationships result in increasing the individuality, pride in accomplishment and self-esteem of each person. We do this by giving daily validations for the things we appreciate in our partners. We provide for each other affirmation of our value as persons, belief in our inherent worthiness and celebration of our unique and special qualities.

All of us are capable of learning the skills that are the keys for successful relationships. At first an unfamiliar skill may seem awkward, but in time it will become second nature. Practicing these relationship skills shows our respect for our partners and is a clear demonstration of our love and commitment to the relationship.

Communication

To develop basic and essential communication skills, we
first need to avoid barriers to communication and then use
good listening and dialogue skills. It's also important to have
a sense of timing and to make the best use of an opportunity
when the survivor is ready and willing to talk about the experience. Try to stick with it and avoid unnecessary interruptions,
drifting off the subject or diverting attention to something or
someone else. Also remember that most survivors must talk
about the experience repeatedly, each time covering just a
little bit more, rather than being pressured into a single, totally
revealing catharsis.

Without intending to block communication, we may fall
into behavior patterns that make it difficult for others to talk
with us. Barriers to communication occur when one person
takes a superior position, refuses to take the other person
seriously or withdraws from the conversation. Each of these
behaviors erects barriers to communication by an implied
attack on the self-esteem of the other person.

Identifying patterns that erect barriers to communication in
our own behavior is more difficult than spotting them in
others. Notice how easy it is to visualize someone we dislike
acting in a way that blocks communication and how hard it is
to see it in our own conduct. All of us have at times done or
said things that block communication, often without knowing
it. We need to practice self-awareness so we can recognize
and eliminate dysfunctional communication styles and attitudes in ourselves.

Based on the work of Thomas Gordon, Parent Effectiveness
Training teaches the use of good listening skills that facilitate
communication and encourage the other person to give full
and free expression to their thoughts and emotions. These
include passive listening, paraphrasing, echoing, active listening, clarifying and open response. Each of these techniques
can be used in different situations to extend and enhance
communication. With a little practice they will become a natural and comfortable way of talking.

Since survivors are subject to flashbacks and recurring memories that may pop up or intrude into the conversation at any time, the survivor may occasionally "space out" or lose track of what is being said. If this happens, a deep breath may be all they need to come back and re-engage in the conversation. Partners and survivors need to give each other permission to ask, "Did you hear what I just said?" or "Excuse me, I wasn't present for a minute. Would you repeat what you just said?" It isn't for lack of interest or failing to pay attention that this happens. Kindly accepting these occurrences without judgment is the best way for partners and survivors to gently let this go without allowing it to become an irritant or barrier to communication.

Dialogue Skills

"I" messages, problem resolution, body language and appropriate touch are key techniques when the conversation moves into dialogue. These techniques are all elements of clear communication.

"I" Messages

"I" messages, another of Thomas Gordon's ideas, are extremely effective because they clearly and logically express the situation, results and feelings in the message. Unlike "You" messages, in which the "you" is often followed by a negative message that erects a barrier to communication, "I" messages put forth the sender's emotion and what gave rise to that emotion. The example, "When I find the kitchen in a mess and I am left to clean it up, then I feel annoyed and unappreciated," follows the "I" message formula:

A. When (situation)
B. And (result)
C. Then I (feeling)

The clearest form of the "I" message begins with a concise and objective description of the situation, follows with a logically connected explanation of the results and their impact on me and concludes with a clear expression of my feelings. The clearest order of the three parts usually follows the natural progression of the situation occurring first, followed by the results and their emotional impact. The order can also be changed as long as all three parts are present. For example: "I fly off the handle when things are scattered in the garage after I have just cleaned up and I have to clean it again."

In phrasing an "I" message it is best to avoid using the word "you." Using the word "you" is likely to provoke an angry or defensive response. This is particularly true when the "I" message is used to communicate a negative feeling. In giving credit and sharing positive emotions, it's okay to use the word "you," particularly in describing the situation. It is never, never acceptable to use the word "you" in the feeling part of the message — i.e., "You make me angry (or happy)" — since we are each responsible for our own feelings.

Problem Resolution

Conflict and problems are inevitable in human relationships, but they need not lead to fighting and further aggravation. In a relationship workshop with Sid and Suzanne Simon, I learned how to stop fighting and start resolving problems. There are three steps that lead to effective problem resolution:

1. Express the underlying feelings
2. Identify the unmet needs
3. Negotiate an acceptable solution

One common mistake is to skip or pass too quickly through the step of expressing the underlying feelings. This is particularly true for partners and survivors from dysfunctional homes where feelings were either not acknowledged or shouted at top voice. Many of us never learned that feelings are not right or wrong, they just are. Even if we have little practice or experience at this, it is worth the time for the ultimate success of the problem-resolution process. Leaving the underlying emotions unexpressed is likely to sabotage the solution when the buried feelings resurface and cause the problem again.

When expressing emotions in a relationship between partner and survivor, it helps to remember that this is a step in the problem resolution process and is intended to lead to a solution acceptable to both. This means making it safe for each of us to be vulnerable. It means taking the risk to be open and real, showing our true inner feelings. Expressing current anger in a nondestructive way is a healthy part of the problem-resolution process and does not mean that the relationship is in trouble.

The second step is to identify the unmet needs that are causing the problem. This should be limited to the needs associated with the immediate problem rather than a catalogue of every conceivable slight in the history of the relationship. Focusing on the real and immediate needs of both sides promotes understanding and eliminates false assumptions. In this step we often find that our needs are more similar than different, promoting an attitude of reconciliation.

In the third step, we listen to each other and consider realistic alternatives that offer a specific solution related to the identified needs. Since the solution deals directly with needs, both partner and survivor are encouraged to clarify and reveal their true needs. Off-the-wall suggestions that confuse the situation can be discarded as not related to the identified needs. Then the problem-resolution process can efficiently proceed to a negotiation of viable alternatives.

Good-faith bargaining means that we are willing to discuss any alternative and that we have not come into the negotiation wedded to a single preconceived solution. The negotiation should give us room for compromise in the search for a cooperative, complementary and reciprocal solution. The end result of a successful problem-resolution process is a solution that resolves the problem and empowers both partner and survivor to place the solution into effect.

This chart contrasts effective problem resolution with nonproductive fighting. By being aware of the negative attitudes and behaviors associated with fighting and envisioning the positive rewards of problem resolution, we can consciously choose to fight less and resolve problems more.

Attitudes That Distinguish Fighting
From Problem Resolution

FIGHT (Win/Lose)	PROBLEM RESOLUTION (Win/Win)
1. Feelings right/wrong attack antagonism mask stuff walls	**1. Feelings** just are safety vulnerability real open risk
2. Needs selfish false assumptions difference retaliation	**2. Needs** two sides understanding similarity reconciliation
3. Solutions shout demand impossible force contrary opposition unilateral compound problem overpower	**3. Solutions** listen consider alternatives realistic compromise complementary cooperation reciprocal resolution empower

Problem resolution is an ongoing process of solving new problems as they come up and refining the solutions to old problems. As circumstances change, an old problem may come up in a new form or an old solution may no longer be workable. Some difficult problems may require negotiating a temporary solution with an agreement to negotiate after a set period. For example, we may agree to try a given solution for one week to see how it works. Whether it is part of the negotiated agreement or not, good problem solvers periodically check old solutions to be sure they are still workable. The problem resolution process is robust enough to respond to any change and allows the solution to be renegotiated at any time.

Body Language

Nonverbal communication is an important skill that can either facilitate or hinder conversation. This includes body posture, eye contact, facial expressions and hand gestures. Although there are some differences in body language due to variations in ethnic and cultural background, we can describe common characteristics.

An open body posture communicates willingness to listen, while a closed body posture generally is interpreted as defensiveness. Openness is shown by uncrossed hands, arms and legs. Clasped hands, folded arms and crossed legs may indicate a closed mind. Inadvisable body positions also include postures that intimidate by placing one person in a superior position. Some of these are standing over someone who is sitting or lying down, puffing up the chest, flaunting the breasts or presenting the genital area or buttocks. A swagger or other exaggerated body movement or walking style may also be read as superior posturing.

Making eye contact and holding it with interest facilitates trust and communication, while dropping eye contact and frequently looking down or away may make it hard to sustain the conversation. Tears are part of the healing process of expressing grief or other strong emotions and should be encouraged rather than suppressed. Looking into each other's eyes can be an intimate and bonding process when it is done with an attitude of openness and willingness to see and be seen. Let your eyes be a window into your true inner being and at the same time a loving mirror of the precious person before you.

Showing emotions through facial expressions can give depth and vitality to spoken expressions of compatible emotions. By the same token, facial expressions may belie false and insincere mouthing of feelings that are not really felt. The facial expressions that facilitate communication include smiling, nodding and similar expressions that indicate open and thoughtful listening. Distancing expressions include frowning, scowling, raising eyebrows, pursing lips, yawning or showing stone-faced indifference.

Resting your head in your hand may be interpreted as a sign of disinterest. Placing a hand in front of your face may be seen as an act of concealment or a barrier to communication. Studies have also shown that open-handed gestures with palms up are preferable to gesturing with a fist or with palms down. Unless it's used to clarify directions, pointing is universally received as a negative, accusatory gesture. Gestures like beckoning and extending open and outstretched arms are seen as an invitation to come closer or to receive a hug.

Appropriate Touch

Human beings need to be touched. We hunger for appropriate and nurturing touch. It is an important part of establishing and maintaining a close relationship that includes intimate communication. From the time we are babies we need to be cradled, cuddled and hugged, and we never outgrow our need to receive physical strokes. It is interesting to note that cats and dogs are able to communicate this need clearly and most of us are unable to resist stroking or petting a friendly cat or dog. In some dysfunctional families the only available nurturing touch was contact with the family pet.

As adults we need to ask for the kind of nurturing touch we need and to offer appropriate touch in return. Sexual abuse survivors are no exception and must face and discuss this issue with their partners. Since inappropriate touch may trigger unwanted memories or a negative response, survivors need to be clear about the kind of touch they want and can accept. Partners need to respect this expression of the survivor's physical boundary. When survivors are first beginning to set limits, define boundaries and build a sense of identity separate from the memories of sexual abuse, they may say no to all touch. But functional boundaries change over time and are flexible to respond to changes in personal need and growth. By continuing to gently offer safe, nurturing touch and invite physical contact without force, partners can assist survivors in moving through the no-touch stage.

Since sexual touch is usually highly charged and confusing for a child, survivors recover slowly and require time to reclaim a sense of sexual identity that includes sexual contact. Part of the recovery process is beginning to learn to refuse unwanted touch and refusing to participate in dysfunctional or undesired sexual behavior. For this reason, partners need to give primary attention to safe, nonsexual touch. This kind of touch is *never* violent, forced, confining or smothering and avoids stimulating breasts, genitals and other erogenous areas. Although every survivor is different, safe and nonsexual touch generally includes holding hands, touching arms or shoulders, stroking hair or back and nonsexual hugging.

To be sure that the touch is safe, the partner can say, "I'd like to give you a hug. Would you like a hug?" This is particularly important if the survivor's abuse included surprise or was initiated in an unexpected sneak attack. Partners and survivors can discuss in advance and periodically restate the kinds of touch the survivor wants, needs and considers safe at the time. Talking about the physical boundary and respecting it is an excellent way to facilitate communication and build trust and intimacy between partner and survivor.

Staying Present

One of the major tasks in recovery for sexual abuse survivors is separating the present from the past. This means cleaning up loose ends and putting past experiences in their proper perspective so they no longer intrude on the present moment. This frees the survivor to experience serenity and happiness, and as far as possible give full awareness in the here and now to a true sense of identity. Having a partner who is grounded in reality and stays present most of the time is beneficial.

Awareness of the now and identity with the present moment are not weighted down by the pain and resentment of the past or inhibited by anxiety and fear of the future. Not being present is like living behind a wall of glass. That wall keeps us from experiencing connectedness and belonging and separates us from contact with reality. It may be helpful to inten-

tionally focus attention on the present moment until it becomes second nature to stay present in the here and now as
much as possible.

Commitment

It is in the safety of a committed relationship with a supportive partner that many survivors find they can risk facing
the core issue of sexual abuse. It is precisely because the
relationship is so good that the survivor can risk bringing up
the negative memories from the past. Usually this must be
done primarily in individual therapy or within a sexual abuse
recovery program. Often this means that the survivor re-expe-
riences the trauma, pain and impact of the sexual abuse,
placing great strain on the relationship. Many partners have
found they can consider it an honor to be the one chosen to
live with the survivor while facing this grievous issue. They
can take this validation as a reason to renew their commitment
to sustain the relationship.

Survivors who continue to feel secure in the knowledge
that the partner values the relationship can continue to pursue
recovery as fast as possible. It is a great comfort for the survivor
to know the partner thinks the relationship is worth whatever
it takes to see it through. It increases intimacy and strengthens
the bond for both partner and survivor to validate each other
for showing commitment to the relationship.

Experience has shown that recovery from sexual abuse
takes time but in almost every case eventually results in improved personal functioning. When the survivor's memories
first start returning, things seem to get worse, and many
partners wonder whether they will ever get better. Not only
must partner and survivor have the commitment to stay together for the duration, they must also commit the time
needed for repeatedly facing the issues. Recovery requires
being willing to put in the time necessary to talk through the
issues as they come up and to talk the same issue through
again and again, as many times as necessary, until it is resolved. This may require making time available or scheduling

time on specific days, after dinner, before bedtime or on weekends for just talking. Both partners and survivors report that time spent on recovery is worth it and has resulted in some of their most meaningful lifetime experiences.

Partners may find that survivors set up situations to test the partner's trustworthiness or commitment to the relationship. Survivors who have had their ability to trust shattered by the experience of sexual abuse may continue to test and push the trust issue, seemingly to provoke another abandonment experience. Partners who experience this repeated testing — particularly those who are set up with secret, impossible and unfair tests — may legitimately feel angry.

> I was sandbagged. She said she wanted flowers for her birthday, so I stopped at the flower shop on the way home. I know she likes roses and carnations so I picked out a mixed bouquet that had one red rose, one white and two pink carnations, some daisies and some other flowers. Then I went home and she put the bouquet in a vase and opened her birthday present, some expensive perfume, but I could tell something was not right. I found out I hurt her feelings because I didn't get a dozen red roses. "If you really loved me, you would have known I wanted roses."

Partners who are forewarned can avoid the trap of turning their anger on the survivor. Instead, they can reassure the survivor of the depth of their commitment and direct their anger toward the abuser who shattered the survivor's ability to trust. The survivor needs to hear that the partner did as well as possible with the information available and that the partner will continue to be as trustworthy and supportive as possible. The partner can reassure the survivor by saying, "I know you have been hurt by others and it was not my intention to hurt you again. I'm on your side and I want to work this through with you. I'm not going to deliberately hurt you or leave you, and I don't want this incident to come between us."

> Last night was a particularly bad night. Nothing was going right. We were each so keyed up there was nothing either of us could do or say without setting the other one off. We were going

over the same old stuff, getting nowhere, and I almost decided to cut and run. I figured, what the hell, I couldn't do any worse. I might as well take my chances with somebody else.

It's a good thing I didn't do anything rash, because today I see things a little differently. What if I started over with somebody else and found out they had been abused too? All of my relationships have been with incest survivors. I attract them like moths to a flame. There must be a sign on my back saying: "Only incest survivors need apply."

It suddenly came to me that leaving would only be delaying things and I'd probably find myself starting over again from the beginning with another survivor. Nothing's going to change if I don't do something about my own issues, and I have a better chance of doing that right where I am.

We both work a good program and support each other. It isn't perfect but we've got a lot of things going for us, and it really is a lot better than it used to be. I've decided to stay and I'd like to say it out loud, right now: "I'm committed. I'm sticking with it to the end."

We as partners can show the survivors we have the staying power to outlast the difficulties and problems. During the recovery process survivors may do some erratic and unpredictable things, testing limits and trying to develop an independent sense of identity. It helps if the partner can be a responsible and dependable counterpart and provide a sense of continuity. Whatever the survivor may do, the partner can supply a stable perspective grounded in reality. Commitment means forming an alliance between partner and survivor to overcome all obstacles to recovery. It means not allowing problems to come between us. Instead, it means staying united against the effects of sexual abuse and finding the solution together.

Flexibility

One of the key characteristics of functional relationships is flexibility. The boundaries are not so rigid that the relationship cannot respond to change, and inflexible rules do not stifle the personal growth of each person. Mature and mentally healthy adults continue to respond to challenges with new ideas and behavior throughout their lives.

Living with a survivor every day can take an unanticipated turn. Life is an adventure full of surprising discoveries and new beginnings. Sometimes there is laughter and delight; sometimes there are tears and hurt feelings. When we are both in the same mood it's great, but when we're out of sync it can be a problem.

It hurts to hear a "No" and be asked to back off. I know it's not me, that she's doing what she has to do to take care of herself, but it still stings. It helps to remember that I'm not the enemy and the "No" is not directed at me personally. Incest is the specter that haunts us and blocks our fun, but we are clever enough to keep trying new ploys until we outflank the demon.

Partners and survivors may face greater than average need for flexibility. Recovery for many survivors means rebuilding a sense of identity by retracing developmental stages, particularly the stages of sexual development, from childhood through youth and adolescence to adulthood. This means boundaries and rules in the relationship must be flexible enough for the partner to accept the survivor's behavior as it changes unpredictably from one developmental stage to another on almost a daily basis. Behavior regression to compensate for incomplete developmental stages occurs in an accelerated time frame. Even with cycling through some stages several times, the total time spent in age-incompatible behavior is not long. Still it is a bit unsettling to tolerate in an adult such behaviors as the flirting, coquettishness and teasing that are characteristic of adolescence.

As survivors begin reclaiming a sense of sexuality and start being able to be fully present during sex, there may be periodic flashbacks that cause them to numb out and call a halt to the sexual activity. To support the mutual goal of having the survivor be fully present during sex, the partner must have the willingness and flexibility to respect the survivor's need to say no. The partner must give the survivor absolute authority to say when to stop and when to proceed.

To avoid specific touch, positions or behavior that trigger flashback memories, the partner and survivor may search for creative alternatives and explore new sexual behaviors that bring satisfaction to both. This requires cooperation and compromise in addition to flexibility. Finding out what works and what doesn't means talking about what you are going to try next and checking it out before proceeding. It helps if both partner and survivor try to be tolerant of each other's needs and quirks and approach the process with a spirit of playfulness and a sense of humor.

Constructive Anger

Anger is one of the most powerful human emotions. When unchanneled or misdirected, it can be destructive to ourselves, others and property. When focused, anger becomes a constructive and useful tool.

Sexual abuse survivors often fear anger because they have repeatedly been its victims and have never seen anger used constructively. Since survivors have usually been the ones with the least power in the abusive situation, their experience with anger is that it only makes things worse. With these types of experiences in mind, it's easy to see why survivors usually cannot allow themselves to become angry or must quickly stifle or dissipate their anger. The submerged pool of anger will remain unconscious, often consuming a large portion of the survivor's mental energy in keeping it contained until something changes that makes it safe to express the anger.

For a survivor who was physically or psychologically overpowered, the risk of showing anger toward the abuser may have been so great that the survivor displaced it onto something or someone else or turned it inward. Since anger displaced or turned inward is not effective in resolving the situation, it will come up again and again until there is a different result. Ultimately the anger must be expressed toward the abuser where it rightfully belongs.

Partners of survivors, who are indirect victims of the abuse, can also appropriately feel angry at the abuser. Partners who have access to their feelings may feel angry with the abuser from the first time they are told. They may find their outrage seems disproportionately large when compared to the weakness of the survivor's anger. The partner may find it easy, almost automatic, to sustain an appropriate level of anger until a solution begins to emerge. It is helpful for a survivor to see the partner's healthy display of anger and to see that nothing bad necessarily results from getting angry. Survivors must come to know that they too have a right to feel angry and direct that anger specifically toward the abuser, not displace it or turn it inward. Usually it is necessary for the survivor to learn to stay with the anger until the full depth of the atrocity has been felt.

> Every time I think about it I get enraged. I'm angry at her mother, I'm angry at her father, I'm angry at the whole family. I'm angry at society for setting it up, I'm angry at the whole world for letting it happen. I'm angry at the perpetrator, I'm angry at the incest, I'm angry that she got hurt and I'm angry because I'm in pain.
>
> I'm tired of hurting and I'm going to do something about it. I'm not going to let those assholes ruin my life. I'm taking charge of me. From this moment on I'm going to do what I want to do and live the way I want to. Nothing that happened before is going to stop me. I'm cutting myself loose from the assholes who have hurt me. I no longer give them power and control over me. I'm going to do whatever it takes to heal myself. I want to find the true me, I want to live the life I was meant to live.

Anger over past injury can be expressed in nondestructive ways. It is particularly effective to cry from the depth of the feeling, letting tears flow. Other healthy expressions of anger include yelling, screaming, roaring or growling. The energy of the anger can then be constructively used to initiate the grieving and healing process. Our anger empowers us as partners and survivors to take whatever action is necessary in our particular situation.

Sensitivity And Gentleness

Partners and survivors can learn to treat each other with exquisite sensitivity and gentleness. Survivors are often particularly sensitive to actions, words, sounds, smells or situations that resemble the abusive situation or environment. Partners may find they have inadvertently done something that presses the survivor's hot button. Partners who are forewarned can be alert to ask what caused the response and to retreat quickly. Survivors can trust the partner to be attentive and sympathetic and can be gentle and forgiving when the partner unintentionally blunders into a sensitive area.

> I learned something about sensitivity at a workshop where we took turns alternately being blindfolded and leading someone who was blindfolded. When I was leading, my blindfolded partner stumbled over door sills and curbs because I didn't remember to alert her to changes in the floor level. I even walked through the middle of the doorway and led her into the door jamb because I forgot she was walking at my elbow, one step to the side. I told myself, "Come on, get it together. Even dogs can learn to guide the blind." Then I started to pay attention and to be sensitive to her needs.
>
> Living with a survivor is something like leading a blindfolded person. Once I learned the cues, there were some obvious things I needed to do or avoid. I tell her what I'm doing in advance so she isn't faced with unpleasant surprises, and I pay attention so I don't stumble into sensitive areas. Choosing to be in a relationship with a survivor means choosing to be sensitive to her issues.

By sharing thoughts and feelings as they come up, partners and survivors can learn to identify and avoid any stimulus that provokes an unpleasant response. At times the partner may feel this is like walking on eggs and that it's hard to be so careful. The survivor, from the other side, may feel this is like being inside the walked-on eggs and that it's hard to be so trusting.

The sympathetic partner learns to be attentive and alert, treating the survivor with compassion. The partner grows to feel empathetic and comes to know intuitively how to avoid pressuring the survivor, when to push onward and when to pull back. Through establishing a consistent pattern of trustworthy behavior, the partner provides the degree of safety that the survivor needs in order to regain an ability to trust.

Nonsexual Intimacy

Intimacy is often confused with sexuality, and the phrase "an intimate relationship" usually implies that it includes sex. Certainly sex can be part of intimacy, but intimacy is much more than that. Since many survivors find it necessary to place a temporary moratorium on sex during part of the recovery process, partners and survivors need to find nonsexual ways to continue the intimacy in their relationships.

Intimate and nurturing touch need not be sexual. For example, offering or asking for a massage that avoids erotic stimulation may be welcomed. This could include massaging head, neck, shoulders, back, legs or feet. Either person could initiate, since both giving and receiving a massage increases feelings of intimacy. Other nonsexual touch includes holding hands, nonsexual hugging, cuddling and tender stroking of the head, shoulders and back. Even after it is possible to resume sexual activity, a healthy intimate relationship will include a large portion of such nonsexual touch. It is wise, however, to avoid initiating sex or sexualizing the intimate touch until the survivor has reached the appropriate point in recovery and has agreed to it in advance.

We have some special words we use when we want to be close without being sexual. For example, we say, "Let's cuddle" or "Just hold me" when one or the other of us doesn't feel like having sex. When we've agreed to cuddle, she can relax and enjoy the nurturing sensations without worrying about sexual advances. Even if she notices that I'm getting an erection from the pleasure of holding her close, she doesn't have to get defensive because she knows I'm not going to act on it. The truth is that I'm enjoying it too, and we both need cuddling a lot more often than we need sex.

Shared physical activity that may or may not involve contact also builds intimacy. The range of possible activities is very broad, including walking, jogging, hiking, bicycle riding and dancing. Any shared interest will do. Even sharing chores like grocery shopping, laundry, housework, and yardwork may increase intimacy.

In addition to touch and physical activity, intimacy includes sharing feelings and ideas. Intimate friends often engage in stimulating and interesting conversations with a free and open exchange of significant thoughts and ideas. This may include friendly arguments or discussions during which they agree to disagree. In addition to an exchange of thoughts, intimate conversations generally include an open and honest sharing of feelings as they come up or soon after. Intimate conversations frequently include catching each other up on the strongest and most significant emotions that have come up since the last talk. Nonsexual intimacy means being real with one another, dropping masks and being vulnerable and unguarded.

Also try putting a little romance in the relationship. Surprise each other now and then with a little unexpected gift. Think of cards, poetry, flowers, candy or something else you know would be appreciated. Arrange for a romantic candlelight dinner at home or a quiet restaurant. Plan a weekend getaway without children and responsibilities at a favorite resort or vacation spot.

Validation

The easiest way to understand validation is to look at its more common opposite — criticism. Criticism or fault-finding is the opposite of validation and has the opposite results. A critic looks for qualities that are faulty or lacking and calls attention to the defect. When human beings are criticized, we internalize the negative descriptors and experience a corresponding loss of self-esteem. Even in constructive criticism, where the fault-finding is coupled with a suggestion for improvement, the result is a lasting memory and feeling of deficit.

Praise is sometimes considered the opposite of criticism, and it is certainly much more positive. Validation is also different from praise. Praise is given as a reward for a particular behavior and is an attempt to motivate or increase that behavior. The praise-giver has an ulterior motive of modifying the behavior of the subject, who recognizes the conditional nature of the praise and attempts to earn that reward again by repeating the behavior. Praise may be given in exchange for cooperation or favors or to elicit praise returned in kind. If praise is the only kind of positive recognition given, it will be perceived as controlling and the receivers will only feel valued for what they can do.

Validation is an unconditional recognition of a positive quality communicated with no motive other than the celebration of another's existence. Validation is a genuine and spontaneous expression of emotion as a free gift with no expectation of return or change in behavior. Whether spoken or written, validations are lovingly given as true admiration or appreciation of qualities exhibited. Validation goes beyond noticing actions or behavior and perceives with reverence and respect another's personality.

Learning to give validation is a skill that comes with practice and may initially be tinged with elements of praise or constructive criticism. In time it will come as second nature to give pure validation freely. Although there is no set formula for validation, it is usually a communication of an "I message" and begins with the word "I." The language of validation continues with an emotion that expresses what you feel: I honor, I cherish, I admire, I applaud, I treasure, I respect, I appreciate, I like, I love.

A validation concludes with a statement of the quality or personality characteristic that prompted the emotion. "Your friendship," "the way you care," "how hard you try," "your cheerfulness," "your patience for just listening," "you for just being you," "how much you've grown," "your persistence" are all examples that may suggest the myriad possibilities. Validations are a search for the good, what we do well, how we enrich life, the best parts of ourselves. Validations are best if given promptly when the emotion is still fresh and both can immediately recall how the quality was exhibited.

A single validation is a small thing, but many given over time strengthen and repair relationships. By building a web of acceptance, approval and support, validations enhance the self-esteem of both sender and receiver. Both partner and survivor can practice validating each other or even giving self-validations at appropriate times.

Affirmation

Affirmation goes hand in hand with validation and extends to the totality of the individual. In their Values Realization workshops, Dr. Sidney and Suzanne Simon practice the use of validations and affirmations to communicate that each person is fully and completely accepted as is. We are affirmed and happy when we feel valued as a person — worthy, important and good enough just the way we are. Affirmation is approval with no strings attached. It enables us to become actualized and to have sufficient self-esteem to realize our potential.

Survivors in recovery need affirmation of their identities and re-affirmation of every new behavior as their true identity begins to emerge and blossom. The partner's affirmation confirms that the survivor is unique and worthwhile as a person. This helps survivors feel lovable and capable in their own as well as their partner's eyes.

It is especially important, *at the appropriate time,* for the partner to notice and appreciate the survivor's returning sense of sexuality. This is generally a gradual process of growing and emerging sexuality that may parallel the initial sexual development of the teenage years. There may be an incremental reclamation of positive body feelings, each of which can be affirmed and appreciated as if it were a new discovery.

When enough affirmations are received and assimilated, survivors will begin feeling self-assured and in full possession of their body most of the time. They will become able to reach out and respond to the needs and demands of the partner and others. It will then become possible for survivors to approach conflict and compromise with a positive, confident and giving attitude.

Specific Support Tasks

As a survivor progresses through the stages of recovery, there are specific tasks that often involve the partner. A partner who understands and expects these to occur can provide the support the survivor needs. Recovery is an individual process that is the responsibility of the survivor, who must remain in control of it. Although the partner wants to be helpful, there must be no pressuring or misguided attempts to hurry the survivor through the process. The partner should be aware that the entire recovery process may take many months or even several years, requiring patience in addition to a desire to be supportive.

Even when the partner can see what task the survivor is working on and feels confident of the type of support the survivor needs, it is still best to ask whether any assistance is wanted. Offer the support, but take the cues from the survivor and be sure to let the survivor remain in control.

Accepting Reality

Loss of memory regarding the sexual abuse is one of its most common characteristics. Many survivors find their first memories are just a general feeling that something was wrong or an anxious feeling something may have happened that is too frightening to fully recall. If someone thinks they may have been sexually abused, they probably were. If there is any indication that the person had a troubled childhood or came from a dysfunctional family, it is best to assume there was sexual abuse until it is definitely proven otherwise.

Believe that it happened and accept it as reality from the moment the survivor opens the subject. It is not helpful to cast any doubts on what the survivor is saying. It is better to assume it is true and support the survivor in checking out the extent of the abuse. Discounting the foggy memories and driving them deeper into unconsciousness only delays recovery. It is the nearly unanimous experience of others that the early inklings of sexual abuse have in fact proved to be true. It is safe to assume suspected sexual abuse is true rather than a fantasy or flight of the imagination that is not grounded in reality.

Be grateful for the level of trust in your relationship that allowed the survivor to tell you of suspicions or memories. It does no good to say, "Why didn't you tell me earlier?" Most survivors move toward recovery as rapidly as they can, given their individual circumstances. If they could move faster, they would. It is much better to say, "I am honored that you trust me enough to share this memory of a distressing experience that must have caused you great pain." Do what you can to be trustworthy and promote a feeling of safety and encourage the growth of trust. Experiences of sexual abuse have shattered the survivor's trust and the ability to trust is not regained easily or quickly.

No matter what the circumstances, the survivor of child-hood sexual abuse is *not to blame.* The responsibility belongs squarely on the abuser, never on the victim. Particularly when the survivor is full of shame and recalls behavior that might have instigated the incident, the partner needs to provide reassurance that the survivor is not at fault. Even if the abuser's personality or position seems to be above suspicion, this does not mean the victim did something to cause it.

What if you as a partner of a survivor of sexual abuse have doubts about what happened, are angry that the survivor did not tell you sooner or think the survivor must have been partly at fault? Work these thoughts through in private with a trusted third party, a counselor or your support group. Do not ignore your doubts, anger and suspicion, or the survivor will be able to sense something is wrong. Do not express these feelings to the survivor, who needs your unqualified support and encouragement. You have a right to your feelings and they need to be expressed, but this should be done elsewhere since they can have damaging consequences if expressed to the survivor.

This is the beginning of the survivor's recovery, and it is likely to be a prolonged process. Although it may seem frightening, it is better to encourage the survivor to get in touch with all the memories and feelings rather than offer comfort with hollow phrases like, "That was a long time ago," "That was then and this is now" or "Let bygones be bygones." It is also a mistake to press for immediate forgiveness or reconciliation with the abuser, no matter what your own feelings or relationship might be with that person. Forgiveness comes in the later stages of recovery, if at all.

Often survivors feel overwhelmed by the feelings that emerge with the first awareness of the sexual abuse. These feelings may include depression, obsession, confusion and waves of terrifying pain. Although survivors sometimes think they are hallucinating or feel as if they are going crazy and losing their minds, this is just a temporary phase that usually does not last long. Some survivors may become suicidal before the intense feelings of this initial awareness decrease. If the survivor becomes suicidal, immediately reach out for assistance. Call a suicide prevention agency, a counselor, or the mental health department for help. Neither the partner nor survivor should attempt to deal with suicidal feelings alone. It should be a comfort for both of you to know that the intense feelings of the emergency stage pass with time.

It is common for survivors to have periodic relapses into denial, during which they doubt the reality of their own abuse. When this occurs the partner can serve as an anchor to reality reminding the survivor, "Yes, you really were abused." Or "What happened to you counts as abuse." "Yes, it *was* that bad." It is not helpful to minimize what happened or compare it with the severity of another's abuse. As more memories return, be prepared to accept the reality of incidents that may seem unbelievable. Even if you could prove that some detail was historically inaccurate, the survivor's perceptions, memories and feelings are absolutely real.

Discontinuing Or Changing Relationships

To facilitate recovery it is often necessary for the survivor to discontinue contact or limit relationships with the abuser and/

or other family members who are still in denial about the abuse. The survivor has the right to decide on the degree of contact that is appropriate. This may change during the course of recovery. The partner's role is to find out how much contact the survivor wants and to support the survivor in that decision.

It is not unusual for some members of the survivor's family to be understanding and supportive and others to remain in complete denial. In this case, the survivor may remain in contact with the supportive family members and ask them not to pass on information to the ones in denial. It's possible to retain close relationships with the family members who are also supportive friends.

It's important for the partner to understand that unwanted contact with nonsupportive family members may impede the survivor's recovery. In the presence of family members in denial who perpetuate old family roles and dysfunctional behavior, the survivor may revert back into a childhood role. In this situation the survivor may feel and act like a powerless child, re-experience the terror of the abuse or shut down feelings. Such unpleasant family visits may precipitate new insights, but can just as easily cause setbacks and the re-entrenchment of old behavior and survival mechanisms. Family members in denial may have to be regarded as toxic persons who are poisonous to the survivor's life and recovery.

Quite often, the survivor must choose to break the family rules by talking about the sexual abuse with family friends and relatives. Survivors need to be able to talk about the reality of their experiences without protecting the abuser's feelings or worrying about the family's reputation. The survivor's recovery is worth blowing the lid off the family secret. And siblings of incest survivors may find the courage to acknowledge that they were also its victims when the survivor starts talking. Survivors usually need to obtain external verification of the abuse through talking about it, even if there is a risk of raising the anger of family members still in denial. It's important to remember that the survivor's abuse was real, even if the survivor is faced by the stone wall of an entire family in denial.

With the permission of the survivor, the partner may choose to continue a relationship with the family members in denial or to serve as a communication channel for any information that must be relayed between the survivor and the rest of the family. In this role, for example, the partner may be able to answer telephone calls or screen letters from the survivor's family.

Whatever the arrangements, the partner must let the survivor take the lead in setting limits on family contact. The partner's role is to support that decision whatever it may be. This may include forfeiting an inheritance or losing monetary support, but the survivor's mental health and recovery is worth more than money.

Supporting The Survivor's Therapy Or Program

Having made a decision to heal and a commitment to recover from the effects of sexual abuse, the survivor is setting out on a journey that will require a great deal of time and energy. It is likely that the survivor will decide to make some changes that also have an impact on the partner. This may include allocating time and money to therapy, decreasing the amount of the survivor's time available to the partner and putting a pinch on their accustomed lifestyle. It is likely that the recovery program will require as much time, attention, and resources as if the survivor had taken on a second job.

I thought she would come home from a therapy session and tell me all about it, but a lot of times she would only say something general like, "It was a good session." Then I found she was confiding things to her therapist that she had never told me. I was hurt and angry. I felt she was betraying our relationship. How could she tell a stranger intimate and personal things that she couldn't tell me?

I was also jealous of the special relationship she developed with her therapist. When something heavy would come up, her first thought was to call her therapist. It was only after she had things settled down and kind of figured out that she would tell me what was going on. It took me a while to get over my jealous reaction. But you know if she had told me first, I wouldn't have known what to do with it. I'm too emotionally involved to be very objective, and I don't have the training to come up with the perceptive insights that she gets from her therapist.

The partner should know that it may be a long haul. There are no quick fixes in recovery from sexual abuse. The cost of therapy may not be covered by medical insurance or may exhaust the maximum benefit available for mental health. In addition to the individual therapy sessions, additional time may be required for group therapy sessions, various types of support group meetings or workshops. Survivors often find that therapy sessions and support group meetings trigger memories of repressed experiences and bring up feelings that continue into the following day. The partner should be aware that this is likely to happen and is an expected part of the healing process. Instead of resenting this as an imposition on the relationship, the partner may choose to view it as an opportunity to talk with the survivor about any insights that occurred during the therapy session or meeting.

> I dread the day after therapy, especially if it was a heavy session. She's likely to be moody and usually doesn't want to be bothered. If she's up to talking, she wants to talk about her stuff. When I try to say what's going on in my life, it's like she doesn't even hear me. If I really need to talk I have to call somebody else.

Most therapists and recovery programs encourage the survivor to keep a journal of significant memories, experiences and feelings. They may also ask for other assignments at various times. These may include additional writing or experiments with new behaviors that may involve the partner. The therapist may also want to see the partner for one or more sessions. The survivor's recovery is facilitated by the partner's cooperation in making time available for writing assignments and participating willingly in joint sessions or in trying a new behavior.

> Over the long haul, I have to agree that her therapy is one of the best things that could have happened to us. When I look at

where she is today and where our relationship is compared to a year ago, there's really no comparison. There's been improvement in every area of our lives: communication, sex, intimacy, family, social activity, energy, you name it. I can't say I enjoyed everything that came up through her therapy, but I would never go back to the way it was before.

The partner should also expect the survivor to buy books that deal with recovery from sexual abuse. In fact, some survivors seem compelled to buy every book available. It may also be noted that having bought a book, the survivor may find it too painful to read or may be able to read only one chapter a month. The survivor may initially feel shame about having a book on this subject and may at first keep it in a hidden place. It is an excellent idea for the partner to also read the available literature on recovery from sexual abuse. Becoming educated on the subject is one of the best ways for the partner to support the survivor's recovery.

Validating The Survivor's Personal Progress

As the survivor progresses through the stages of recovery, there will be many significant changes which will have profound effects in the survivor's life and in the relationship with the partner. The partner must be prepared to change along with the survivor if the relationship is to remain viable through recovery. This means noticing the changes the survivor is experiencing and responding appropriately.

The survivor is likely to experience a cycle of feelings during recovery — including pain, sadness, self-blame, guilt, shame, anger and depression — before acceptance and integration can occur. The progression through this cycle of feelings is not even and uniform. The survivor may get stuck at one stage or may express the same few emotions over and over before moving on. The entire cycle may also be repeated as more memories emerge or as a new issue surfaces that has not been previously resolved. Sometimes an issue that has been dealt with before comes up to be worked through again at a deeper level.

In the survivor's preoccupation with recovery and the confusion over newly emerging issues and feelings, the partner may be accused of being the cause of the turmoil. If this happens, don't take it personally. The things the survivor is saying are more about the memories and feelings of the past sexual abuse experience than they are about current interactions in the relationship. Allow the survivor to express negative feelings, but also let them flow over you like water off a duck's back. Take on only the feelings that are directly and immediately related to your current behavior. At the same time, it is also important to notice what the survivor is experiencing and to respond with appropriate validation.

During the emerging memory stage, survivors may have vague and general feelings, dreams that are not clear, foggy visual images, confused auditory responses, unpleasant body sensations, adverse reactions to smells and other types of partial memories. Eventually they will recall more specific incidents and greater numbers of incidents with increasing detail. Survivors may also encounter flashbacks triggered by current life events that are unconsciously associated with memories of sexual abuse. The denied and repressed feelings associated with each memory will also emerge, at the same time or a little later. The partner's role in this stage is to acknowledge the reality of the memories and validate the feelings of pain, betrayal and exploitation as they come up.

Emotional numbness is a common experience of survivors who have not yet been able to allow repressed memories and feelings to return. At first survivors may feel more pain, compassion and indignation over a newspaper account of an unknown person's sexual abuse than for their own. Survivors are often so emotionally distanced from their own experiences that they have more intense feelings for a stranger than they do for themselves. By showing compassion, shedding tears or expressing other appropriate emotions for the survivor's experience, partners may be able to demonstrate how the feelings can be released. This helps give survivors permission to get in touch with their own feelings. Partners can validate both survivors' feelings about the sexual abuse experiences and the difficulty of re-experiencing those terrifying emotions. This is a vital step in the recovery process.

Most survivors have some degree of self-blame or feeling of responsibility for causing or not stopping the sexual abuse. This may come up in thoughts like, "If only I had worn different clothes, if only I hadn't gone there, if only I had said no, if only I had told someone." Even when no one else is blaming them but is saying, "It wasn't your fault," survivors may have adopted an inward sense of condemnation or feeling of worthlessness. These feelings of shame have convinced some survivors that they deserved to be treated with disrespect and abuse. The partner must remain absolutely clear that the survivor is not to blame and did nothing to deserve such abusive treatment. The partner can hold up the image of the survivor as blameless and deserving of respect until the survivor can also reclaim a positive self-image.

Sexual abuse is a betrayal, a personal attack, a destruction of trust and a loss of innocence that the survivor must grieve in the recovery process. Grief includes expressing the emotions of anger, righteous indignation and depression, often in recurring cycles until all of the damage has been grieved. The partner should know that where there has been a lot of damage, there must also be a lot of grief. Supporting the grieving process means validating the feelings each time they come up. The grieving process may seem to take a long time for some survivors, but continued support for progress is the best way to facilitate completion of the grieving and mourning stage. Only if the survivor seems to be stuck in grief, with no sense of long-term progress, should the partner remind the survivor that it is possible to heal and that recovery is a process of slowly making lasting positive changes.

Inner healing means getting in contact with the child within, honoring the pain and reparenting the child until the damage is repaired. Often survivors who have been abused over a period of years have multiple inner children and each must be given attention and gently healed. Ultimately the goal is to get in contact with the undamaged inner child and reclaim the high sense of self-esteem and personal worth that was our birthright. Each of us came into this world whole and undamaged; we were once fully acceptable and worthy just the way we were. Most of us are unfamiliar with the whole and worthy sense of self that is possible when we are in contact with the unified, healed and undamaged child within. Partners and survivors can support each other together in the journey to reclaim the true inner child.

In the later stages of recovery, when the healing process is well under way, some survivors find a new sense of spirituality. This may be through traditional religion and meditation or other personal expressions of spirituality. Since many survivors were abused and neglected by their parents or were not appropriately nurtured and protected, they may have difficulty with traditional religious concepts that use the image of a loving parent. Through the experience of reparenting ourselves and getting in touch with our inner child, some of us have been able to reclaim a belief in a loving higher parent and become reconciled with the religion of our childhood. Partner and survivor alike may find that comfort and growth come with open sharing of spiritual experiences each has experienced during the process of recovery.

The healing, renewed sense of spirituality and sense of wholeness that come at the end of the recovery process make it possible for some survivors to experience forgiveness. In this context, forgiveness means to relieve yourself of resentment and move on. It does not mean forgetting historical facts, letting the abuser off the hook or giving inner peace or anything else to the abuser. It does mean removing the charge from the memories associated with the abuse and the abuser so the survivor can rise above the past.

A survivor who has forgiven will have less energy tied up in their identity as a victim of sexual abuse and can resume living as a whole person. The survivor will be able to say, "I was abused, but I am not my abuse." It is a serious mistake for the partner to push for or even suggest forgiveness at any point early in recovery. The partner should only support the possibility of forgiveness after the anger and grief stages have been substantially completed and healing is well under way.

Accepting New Behavior

If as a partner you have committed yourself to being involved with the survivor's recovery, then you will be affected by all the small changes that happen along the way. When personal growth occurs in successful relationships, both individuals grow together or they will grow apart. If one is growing and changing and the other is not, then one will outgrow the other and it is very unlikely that the relationship will survive. The recovery of a sexual abuse survivor often has a profound impact on the survivor's behavior in a relationship. The committed partner must be prepared to acknowledge and respond with appropriate change.

Early recovery is marked by gradually rebuilding the survivor's ability to trust. As this occurs, the partner is likely to experience corresponding growth in ability to trust and be trustworthy. It's almost as if the growth of the partner is a mirror image of the growth of the survivor. The survivor risks sharing recovery and the partner risks being involved. As the survivor changes in recovery, the partner is invited to grow in response; and as the partner grows, the survivor is encouraged to keep pace. Both partner and survivor can take credit for their many small successes and should periodically note and applaud their personal growth and their progress together.

Growth and behavior change for partners and survivors occur in many areas of personal functioning. We develop an increasing confidence in the validity and reliability of our perceptions, sensory feelings and physical sensations. Our intuitions will reinforce our thoughts, beliefs and feelings as reliable guides for our actions. The emotional numbness that isolated us is replaced by an enhanced ability to experience and express feelings. We are able to ask for help when we need it and to reach out to others who can help us or who need our help. An emerging sense of sexuality renews our interest in sex and our ability to engage in responsive sexual behavior. We see situations that used to frighten us in a realistic perspective that frees us to re-evaluate and change our responses. With the discovery of our inner child and true self comes a sense of high self-esteem and feeling of worthiness.

We regain an ability to trust that allows us to lower our masks and be intimate and real with each other. Coming to terms with our past allows us to be present and aware of our current reality. We find guiding principles that give us the balance and stability needed to live happy, playful and responsible lives. Compassion for ourselves and all human beings restores our belief that there is meaning in life. We are able to understand our personal experience as part of a universal order.

What was in it for me? Well, number one was learning to set limits and establish healthy boundaries. I'm learning to say "No" when she pushes me to engage in dysfunctional and unhealthy behavior. I'm learning to accept a "No" when she cannot accommodate my wants and needs.

I'm learning about the flexibility of physical boundaries. Sometimes she wants and needs to be held, touched, nurtured and cuddled. Other times she cannot accept touch. I'm learning to tell one situation from the other.

Sometimes she's open to moving from nonsexual hugging and cuddling to sexual touch, and sometimes she's not. We are learning how to invite this of each other and how to accept either a positive or a negative response.

Emotional boundaries are similarly developing. We are learning how to feel, express and share emotions without judgment. We can each accept the other as we are and love each other for our similarities and our differences. We don't both have to have the same feelings about every situation.

I'm learning about intimacy that goes beyond sex. We share with each other our problems, issues, successes, failures and insights. We support each other's growth. I know she is working as hard on her issues as I am on fixing mine. I know that for each of us to take care of our own issues is the greatest gift we can give to each other.

Partners who stick with it will find the survivor's recovery was worth it. The benefits for the partner may be as significant as the survivor's recovery. Many partners have found they were challenged to grow in unexpected ways with surprising results. Partners have found a profound love for the survivor, a deeper sense of intimacy and closeness, and a dramatic improvement in the quality of the relationship.

5

Problem Areas

Although there are rewards as the result of living with a survivor, it is also hard work. A number of specific issues that come up again and again directly involve the partner, often causing problems. While each issue may not come up in every relationship, they occur often enough to deserve special attention. These are the areas where we might get stuck and need outside help.

If a problem area comes up more than a few times, outside assistance is probably needed. Find an appropriate resource and use it. Read a book, talk to a friend, join a support group, get into therapy for yourself. Honestly searching for an answer will lead to the right solution for your problem situation.

Why Not Let It Be

Sometimes partners wonder why the survivor can't just let it be, why the survivor can't let bygones be bygones and forget about it.

71

It was such a long time ago, it only happened a few times and it wasn't all that bad. How could it have done so much damage? It seems like she was happier and better off before digging into it. I sure was. I used to have a cheerful and happy wife, now I'm not sure what I've got. You know everybody's been hurt sometime. Why not just forgive and forget?

If it were that easy, the survivor would have done it long ago. The reason it's coming up and the reason it's got to come up is that, underneath the surface happiness, the survivor has been hurting and depressed. Stuffing it hasn't worked very well so far and won't work forever either. The inner suffering won't just go away. What partner would really want the survivor to paste a happy smile on a life filled with pain?

Every survivor has a hidden part that contains the repressed or suppressed feelings and memories of the sexual abuse. These form part of the shadow self containing our negative side that is too private to share with anyone else. We ourselves are often afraid to glance at it for more than a moment and may not know its full extent. The unconscious demons grow stronger when ignored and become weaker when exposed to the light of conscious therapeutic attention. The survivor's repressed or suppressed experiences eventually grow so strong that they intrude into daily life and can no longer be ignored.

Once we as partners see that the survivor's sensitivity and pain are the result of unsuccessfully trying to contain the devastating effects of sexual abuse, we can accept the necessity of dealing with them. Like a boil that must be lanced or a festering wound that cannot heal, the virulent effects of sexual abuse must be treated before the pain can abate. Memories of sexual abuse are like an active infection that continues to break through the scab until it is exposed and disinfected.

The diagnosis many counselors use for victims of sexual abuse is PTSD (Post-Traumatic Stress Disorder), the same diagnosis that has been used for Vietnam veterans and other victims of disaster. Victims of sexual abuse often have many of the characteristics first described and documented for combat

veterans. These include flashback memories, emotional numbness, hypervigilance and feelings of guilt and shame.

When an event such as an experience of sexual abuse
raises more feelings than can be tolerated, the survivor reacts
by quickly entering into denial. If the stress is dealt with in a
healthy manner, this denial is interrupted from time to time by
the unexpected upwelling of emotions. In effect the survivor
processes the experience with an internal pendulum, which
swings freely back and forth between denial of the feelings
and the intrusion of the feelings into awareness. As long as the
pendulum is free to swing, the sexual abuse victim eventually
resolves the stressful experience without a lasting wound.
This is how childhood accidents and other traumatic events
are resolved in healthy and functional families.

PTSD develops when there is no support for healthy resolution and the survivor's normal coping mechanisms are con-
fronted with abnormal levels of stress. This overwhelms the
survivor's ability to break the experience down into digestible
bites. The pendulum that is supposed to swing freely either
gets stuck in the denial or the intrusive phase or else makes
wild swings between the two. Acknowledging the wounds of
sexual abuse a little at a time enables the survivor to free up
the internal pendulum, alternating between denial and intrusion until the stress from the experience is completely resolved. The grief-stricken survivor must mourn bit by bit, not
all at once. To attempt catharsis brings a flood of traumatic
memories with it, creating intolerable levels of anxiety. Grief
remains unabated until the mourning process is undertaken
and completed in small steps.

As partners, we come to understand that our survivors have
unfinished business. It will continue to come up until it is
faced and dealt with in a manner that allows healing to occur.
We understand this means it will take time until all of the
memories emerge and the whole truth is known, and this will
be followed by a period of time when the feelings occur or
recur and intrude into our daily life. The survivor's memories
will continue to interfere with life until they have been talked
out and drained of emotional charge. Only then can the survivor let them be and experience true and lasting happiness.

Both Survivors Of Sexual Abuse

Often both individuals in the relationship are survivors of
sexual abuse. Therefore, both are also partners of survivors of
sexual abuse. Each person will take the roles of partner and
survivor at different times. Such partners can be mutually
supportive or can take turns offering each other support, but
there are some pitfalls to avoid.

The person in crisis or whose abuse was most recent or
most severe more often takes on the survivor role. The less
damaged mate may be reluctant to take the survivor role and
ask for support.

> We are both survivors of sexual abuse, but compared to her, I
> can hardly consider myself damaged at all. I feel I have to put my
> issues on hold and always be there for her. When do I get a turn?

No matter how severely a survivor has been damaged, there
will be times when that person can be supportive to someone
else. There may even be issues or areas where they are particularly strong. It is an important part of recovery for severely
damaged survivors to see how their experience can benefit
others. Let the survivor hear the request for support; the response may be highly comforting.

Since two survivors may have many experiences and feelings in common, there is a tendency to exaggerate the degree
of similarity. It is important to remember that each survivor
has their own experience and their own identity.

> I know exactly how she's feeling and I can tell how she will
> react to every situation. I know what she likes and dislikes. I
> know who she feels comfortable with and who she can't stand.
> On the inside we're just the same.

No two individuals have had exactly the same experience
and no two persons always have the same feelings. Over-
identification with each other and adopting each other's feel-

ings is an invasion of emotional boundaries. If this is a problem, look carefully for the differences and give great respect to the separate identities and distinctions you find.

Don't assume that you know what another person is thinking or feeling without asking in plain language. Don't assume that someone else knows what you want them to know until you have stated it. Neither partner always knows what the other is thinking, feeling, how they will act, what they will accept or reject until it is communicated.

Two survivors may not be able to support each other without getting enmeshed in each other's issues.

> I've always been in a relationship with a survivor, in fact I've never had a relationship with anyone who wasn't. We all seem to be both partners and survivors, and if you're a survivor I don't think I want to have anything to do with you. My last relationship was so bad that I totally lost it. It felt like I was getting hit 24 hours a day with issues coming from everywhere. I lost myself. I only wanted to work it out with her in secret, behind closed doors in whispers, not in group, not with a therapist. It was really sick. I don't think two survivors can work it out together, at least not me. The safest place is with a therapist.

It may not work to stay together, and separating may be necessary to stop the enmeshment and co-dependency. If a separation is necessary, don't take it out on yourself or on each other. Just accept that you each need an outside source of support. There's no blame or guilt in not being able to meet all of each other's needs.

Co-dependency

Partners who are aware of survivor issues are prone to co-dependent behavior. The primary characteristic of co-dependency is a preoccupation with another's problems to one's own detriment. For partners it is hard not to see the survivor's problems as deeper or more significant and to fall into the trap of considering the survivor's recovery to be more important.

When she told me, I was excited — *of course* I was excited about her therapy and the work she was doing. I lost myself completely in her issues. I started reacting to everything she reacted to, and I felt like I had to fix it. I've been a real good friend for two years, totally supporting her program. I know I'm a "co" because I'd rather deal with her stuff than my own. In fact I'm not even sure what my needs are. It gets better when I take care of myself, but keeping the focus on myself is the last thing I feel like doing.

Co-dependent attitudes lead to caretaking behavior that ultimately is not helpful for either survivor or partner. Excessive caretaking prevents survivors from experiencing their own reality: discovering the consequences of their actions, taking responsibility for their decisions, learning from their mistakes and taking credit for their successes. The partner's caretaking may initially be done voluntarily and almost without noticing, but eventually it will lead to feeling resentful and bitter. This creates an impasse where the survivor cannot see what is wrong and the co-dependent partner is filled with resentment.

While falling into co-dependent behavior patterns oneself is not desirable, neither is the opposite — encouraging the survivor to act in co-dependent ways toward the partner. Demanding that the survivor focus on the problems, wants and needs of the partner detracts from the survivor's ability to manage their own recovery. Both the partner and the survivor need to guard against co-dependent or counter-dependent behavior.

To avoid co-dependency, the first rule is to take care of yourself. By keeping your own wants and needs foremost, you know immediately when they conflict with another's. There will inevitably be conflicting wants and needs and at each point there must be a decision whether to yield. Each person should yield at times and prevail at times. If the same person always yields or always prevails, there is something wrong.

A partner may ask, "If it's co-dependent to submerge my wants and needs for the sake of the survivor, does that mean I can't be supportive without being co-dependent?" Of course it's okay to be supportive, offering support as a free gift or doing a favor with a clear understanding regarding the expectation of a return favor. One question to ask yourself is, "If I do this, will I feel resentful?" If possible, avoid doing anything that will build resentment.

If your wants and needs as a partner are not being satisfied, it is probable you are not making them known. It is also possible that you don't clearly know what your wants and needs are. In either case, the survivor cannot be expected to yield to something unknown or unexpressed. Putting your wants and needs forward as facts, but not demands, allows the survivor to respond and say which can be met and which can not.

In choosing to remain in a relationship with survivors who have suffered some degree of damage, partners must be aware that their needs will not always be satisfied. Survivors acting in good faith will try to meet the needs they can to the extent possible and will decline to attempt the ones that would be too painful. Seeing that the survivor has done as much as possible, the partner can take what is available as enough and count the wants and needs as fully met. This is one of the keys to avoiding resentment.

Co-dependency often turns on the issue of who is in control. Survivors frequently have a strong need to remain in overt or covert control — a natural and expected consequence of the abuse they could not control. As the survivor gradually learns to relinquish control in safe circumstances, the control issue is resolved.

Partners can facilitate survivors' recovery from control issues by avoiding a direct confrontation over control in the relationship. Fighting over control is likely to result in re-entrenchment of the survivor's belief that "I get hurt when I give up control." A partner's seizing control, show of force or going on a "power trip" is also likely to have negative consequences.

Instead, the partner can allow the survivor to have control for now while retaining a claim for a more equitable division of control in the future. For example, a partner might say, "I know you're afraid of my driving on winding mountain roads, so why don't you drive until we reach the valley." Or, "You choose the restaurant this time, and we'll go to my choice another time." It costs very little for the partner to give up temporary control over minor areas. The result is promoting a feeling of safety that allows the survivor to move more rapidly to a trusting and equal sharing of control.

If you as a partner find an important issue or area of control where yielding would cause resentment, discuss with the survivor why it is important to you. Seizing control without warning or explanation is very threatening to survivors. As a rule, they do not like surprises in the area of control.

If partner and survivor have conflicting control issues, try negotiating. Today we do it your way, tomorrow we do it my way. You choose in the area that is most important to you and I choose in the area that is most important to me. Let's look for alternatives until we find one acceptable to both of us.

Exhaustion

Exhaustion from the intensity of the recovery process is natural for both partner and survivor. Exhaustion for partners is a signal to take care of themselves, to restore themselves rather than doggedly support the survivor at all costs. For the survivor, a resting time may be necessary to allow inner healing to catch up or to gather energy for the next courageous step. Allowing each other time and space for inner restoration is the key to success during periods of exhaustion.

The time to act is when the feeling of exhaustion begins to emerge, not after total exhaustion has taken over. Exhaustion is a sign to get the rest or support you need. Waiting too long before taking a rest or asking for help can build resentment or have other damaging consequences that are worse than putting things on hold and taking a break.

> When something comes up for her, she reacts, then I react to her reaction and all this garbage starts coming down. I feel a rage coming on and I'm not going to be able to stop it. I've got all these feelings of my own and I can't take it. I yell, "I'm out of here! I'll be back in 20 minutes."

Partners need to remember that they didn't cause the abuse, they are not responsible for fixing it and they couldn't fix it if they wanted to. Listening, offering support and just being there is burden enough and gets tiring after a while. At such times partners need to communicate what is going on with them and take a break. The extent of the break (five minutes, an hour, a day or a week) depends on the degree of exhaustion and the time needed for restoration. Activity during a break may include going for coffee, taking a walk, playing sports, seeing a movie, visiting friends or taking a vacation. Also consider taking a break together and making the topic of recovery off limits for a time if both of you are feeling exhausted at the same time.

If you need a break, don't just leave without saying something. In the absence of clear communication, survivors may take responsibility for causing the disappearance and believe they did something wrong or that something is wrong with them. Also avoid placing blame. Say, "I'm tired of talking right now and I need to take a walk" rather than, "Your story is driving me up a wall." Remember that the survivor has already been unjustly blamed for causing the abuse and doesn't need to be blamed for trying to recover from it.

It's natural for a partner to feel a variety of feelings, including exhaustion and frustration from supporting the survivor. These feelings need to be discharged elsewhere rather than being dumped back on the survivor. A support group for partners of sexual abuse survivors would be ideal. These feelings can also be taken to other group meetings, group therapy, counseling or support networks. Don't try to shoulder the burden alone, but get outside support for yourself and encourage the survivor to do the same.

You may feel like the only friend and source of support the survivor has and feel guilty for needing to take a breather. For long-term recovery, however, the survivor will need to develop a support system and not rely on a single person for support. Taking a break may be what the survivor needs to reach out to others for support.

A false sense of pride gives some partners the idea that they are exclusively responsible for the survivor's recovery and are the only ones who can truly understand and support the survivor in the right way. The truth is that the survivor needs many sources of support and you as the partner should learn to welcome them. The partner needs to let go of exclusivity and allow others to enter the survivor's support system.

When the survivor reaches the point of exhaustion and needs to rest, the partner can change the type of support offered and help the survivor by maintaining a safe haven or resting place. How long the survivor needs to rest varies from situation to situation and survivor to survivor. Some survivors need longer than others, and some issues take longer to assimilate.

Be sensitive to the survivor's needs and allow time to recuperate. Sometimes it seems that the survivor has reached a plateau or is stuck, but generally there is inner healing going on that is a necessary part of preparing for the next step in recovery. Once the last issue has been internally assimilated, the survivor may need encouragement to tackle the next one. Recovery from sexual abuse takes great courage and there is naturally some fear and reluctance to re-enter the struggle after a period of rest. Gently encourage the survivor to take small risks and renew the commitment to recovery.

Children

If children are not already on the scene, there is the question of whether to have them. Many survivors are reluctant or unwilling to have children or seriously doubt their ability to be adequate parents. Some survivors feel pressure from partners or other family members to have children. There is no one right answer. The partner and survivor need to talk over this issue until they can make a choice that feels comfortable.

Given the variety of circumstances and types of relationships, the choice to have children may present an additional set of issues. Most survivors do have the inherent capacity to be good parents despite fears to the contrary. The fact that they are aware of their issues and are choosing recovery only strengthens the likelihood of being good parents.

I'm not sure I have what it takes to raise children. My parents did such a lousy job; I just want to protect my kids from what I went through. I know I'm screwed up by the way I react to children misbehaving in the supermarket. I think, "I wish that kid would *shut up!*" or "What that kid needs is a good spanking." I'm afraid of what I'm going to do to my own kids.

Once children arrive, the parenting process begins whether we are ready for it or not. Since many of us have not had good models in our own parents, it may be advisable to get some parenting training. Many churches, schools and health departments offer training in parenting or parent effectiveness. These are excellent resources that are well worth considering. There are also excellent books on child development and parenting available in libraries and bookstores.

Partner and survivor need to discuss division of childcare responsibilities. Relationships are rarely successful if all the childcare burden falls on one person. Both partner and survivor need to assume an appropriate share of that responsibility. Survivors can have children and continue to work on their recovery at the same time. The survivor's progress in recovery may affect the division of childcare responsibilities. If the survivor is in crisis or is dealing with a heavy issue, the partner may have to temporarily assume a larger share.

Some survivors may have painful memories triggered by contact with children, particularly those the same age as the survivor during the period of sexual abuse. This may happen with one's own children or other children. Sometimes, rather than having clear memories, the survivor just feels uncomfortable around children who look or act in a particular way. This need not be a cause for rejecting or avoiding children. Instead, it can be viewed as an opportunity for growth so the survivor can reclaim the ability to relate with children.

Once children are old enough to know and understand, they should be given an honest explanation of the survivor's situation. Most children become aware that something isn't quite right, but they don't exactly know what it is. A simple acknowledgment of the problem and brief explanation of the recovery meetings and therapy are all that is required. Children do not need to know every detail and it would be inappropriate to tell them, but it is healthy for children to know that adults have problems too and that adults can get help with those problems. Remember that keeping secrets is one of the characteristics of dysfunctional families. Keeping the secret often causes as much damage or more than the problem itself.

Since physical or emotional violation is one of the characteristics of sexual abuse, survivors may have a confused sense of boundaries in these areas. Pay attention to maintaining clear generational boundaries with children. Children should not be exposed to the sight or sound of adult sexuality and should not become the emotional confidant of a parent. These are boundary violations that can lead to physical or emotional incest.

Join a parenting support group. Talk about your parenting experiences with other parents. Find out how they have handled problem situations. Ask for suggestions or advice when you're uncertain.

Protect your children from sexual abuse by educating them. Tell them about good touching and bad touching. Explain their right to privacy. Make sure they know their right to say no even to a parent, step-parent or other adult. Tell them no one has the right to touch them in a way that makes them feel uncomfortable. Do not leave them unattended or inappropriately supervised. Know where your children are at all times, their daily activities, their friends and their friends' parents. Be alert to older children, teenagers or adults who take an unusual interest in your children or give them gifts. Let your children talk. Encourage them not to keep secrets. Pay attention if they say they do not like to be with someone; there may be a reason. Never belittle your children's fears, concerns or anxiety. Be sensitive to changes in behavior or attitude. And believe what they tell you.

Sex

Sexual functioning is perhaps the most sensitive issue for survivors in recovery from sexual abuse. Partners are also intimately involved with this issue. At the beginning of most relationships, the survivor is blocked to sexual abuse issues or in denial about their effects. Sex is usually great when the relationship is new and before the survivor's sexual abuse issues have emerged. In the early recovery stages as memories and issues are emerging, most survivors shut down sexually. It's not uncommon for a survivor to say something like, "I love my husband and I want to have sex, but I just can't do it any more than about once every two months." There is a wide range in the level of sexual activity that survivors can tolerate during recovery.

Being with a survivor was not my conscious choice. I didn't ask for this and I didn't bargain for this. What I thought I was getting and what I got have turned out to be two different things. At the beginning of our relationship sex was frequent, hot and passionate. It was very satisfying for both of us. We agree about this and want to recover what we once had.

After the death of her father, the vividness and immediacy of the memories returned and seriously affected our sex life. When we first come home from work or meet at lunch, she feels sexy and says she wants me. But later in the evening she goes to bed and falls asleep before I get there or stays up so late that I fall asleep. Other times she gets up in the morning before I wake up or stays asleep so long that I give up and get on with my day.

Sometimes when we start making love, she brings up some-thing like our unpaid bills that is sure to set me off and sabotage any chance for an intimate and satisfying sexual experience. If I stop she says she wants to go on, but she won't stop talking long enough for me to believe it. There are some times when she wants to make love but is slow getting started. At first she says that her body feels like lead and her legs just won't move. If we take it easy she starts to open up, and once she gets past a certain point everything starts to flow.

Sometimes we have great sex; the next time I do everything the same and she says I'm pushing her. So the next time I'm very tender and gentle and that works for a while, until she complains that I don't love her any more because the passion and fire isn't there like it used to be. I feel like I just can't win. One day she likes my earthy and manly smell; another day she insists that I shower, brush my teeth and we change the sheets. I tell you it's confusing.

There is little energy available for sex in the initial stages of recovery when the survivor's memories are returning along with the flood of associated feelings. Since early recovery requires the survivor's limited supply of energy to be focused on the emerging memories and feelings, a lack of desire and interest in sex is to be expected. After the discovery of the full extent of the sexual abuse and after the impact of the discoveries has abated, there will eventually be a resurgence of interest in sex.

The trauma and pain of the sexual abuse experience is usually associated with sex in the survivor's mind. Many survivors are only able to have sex by shutting off feelings and numbing out their bodies. Some survivors may find it frightening to contemplate having sex for the first time without alcohol or drugs to numb the emotional pain. As survivors in recovery learn to accept feelings and pay attention to bodily sensations, it's not surprising they hesitate to participate in something that has been associated with mental and physical pain. It takes time to uncouple the survivor's current sexuality from the painful memories of the past.

Survivors have difficulty opening up completely to the magical inner communion of a full sexual experience for fear of getting hurt. Sensitive partners also have difficulty entering unreservedly into the sexual experience for fear of causing hurt. To reclaim full and healthy functioning, survivor and partner must work together to weave a trusting and trustworthy sexual relationship. Building on what feels safe and comfortable, small risks gradually expand the range of possibilities.

Taking small risks agreeable to both has the greatest probability of success, but any risk also includes the possibility of a negative outcome. The important thing is not to stop trying. Try a smaller step, try going more slowly, try something else.

> I've been rejected in initiating sex so often that I don't feel like trying anymore. I really believe I'm a gentle and sensitive lover, but I'm beginning to doubt myself and think there must be something wrong with me. She says she's still interested, but I don't know if I can keep taking the rejection.

The partner's challenge is not to take it personally when rebuffed by the survivor. The survivor's goal is to be gentle in dissuasion of the partner's advances. Both partner and survivor need to remember that the survivor's reaction comes more from the conditioned response to the sexual abuse than from a direct response to the partner's stimulus.

> I know it's not me, but I still can't help taking it personally. It feels like she is rejecting me. I feel shame because I think I should be able to do it right, and she feels guilty because she can't meet my needs. I get my feelings hurt and shut down sexually too, until the next time.

Talking it over is the key to understanding what happened, what is happening and what is likely to happen during present and future sexual activities. Even talking about sex can be risky, and approaching the subject is sometimes easier if it is done at a time or place that does not allow for sexual activity. Talking across a table at a coffee shop may work better than talking in the bedroom.

It is usually not too threatening to ask each other, "What times were best for you?" and "What kind of touch do you like most?" It is also useful to find out what didn't work. Knowing about each other's past experiences usually helps to establish a base of sexual activities that feel comfortable to both of you.

To establish a common goal for the future, it is helpful to find out each other's concept of the ideal sexual relationship. How often would each of you like to have sex if all other problems were solved? What kind of sexual activities, with whom and for how long? Describe the feelings that would happen during an ideal sexual experience.

Many survivors have a distorted and negative view of sex based on old childhood messages and the hurtful abuse experience. It may be difficult for a survivor to visualize anything other than being overpowered, victimized or used. To counteract negative images it is valuable to set forth a positive image of sex. At its best — not always every time — sex is an experience that combines pleasurable touch like being massaged or caressed, enjoyable physical activity like tennis or dancing, emotional closeness like a feeling of oneness or mystical union and a spirit of exhilaration like skiing or a roller coaster ride. Yielding control and letting go to be swept away in the experience is also part of a completely fulfilling sexual experience.

If partner and survivor can share past sexual experiences and future ideals, then it is also possible to talk about current preferences. I can say what I like and listen to what you like. I can understand what feels safe and comfortable to you right now, what you might be willing to try and what we need to avoid. We can find a way to agree on what our sex life will be like. Our goal is to increase our repertoire of activities in which sex plays the role of increasing our bonding, love and intimacy. Intercourse and orgasm are not our only alternatives.

In setting forth the kinds of activities and experiences I would like, I am not placing demands on you. I am willing to be vulnerable and risk getting hurt by saying which things are the most important to me. If you cannot meet my requests, you are still an important and worthwhile person. My love for you remains undiminished.

When I listen to your sexual wishes, I do not necessarily agree to all of them. I am not rejecting you when I tell you what is not acceptable to me. Whether we agree or not, it is a joy for me to get to know who you are.

I am willing to negotiate over the sexual activities we can share. Even if I cannot meet them, I am willing to address all of the things that are most important to you. If something is important to me, you may be able to offer me a close alternative, the next best thing. We can continue talking until we have come to agreement on what we can do with and for each other.

If the relationship is not a committed or closed one, what outside possibilities are acceptable?

Is it okay if one or both partners masturbate?
How often?
Is it okay in the presence of the other partner?
Is mutual masturbation okay?

What about erotic literature or videos?
Are they okay if not pornographic?
If pornographic but not degrading or illegal?
Is it okay to use a vibrator or other erotic device?
What about outside affairs?
Affairs that do not include intercourse?
Outside affairs with safe sex only?

There are no right or wrong answers here. Good relationships can have different answers as long as the answer is okay with both persons.

Whether outside possibilities are allowable and what they are is also subject to change. Keep talking and checking it out. Is the status quo still okay? Things change. One good suggestion is to talk things through first. Acting first and explaining later may have unpredictable consequences.

Regarding sex as an area open for exploration is a healthy attitude for survivors and partners. Keep your eyes open for what you might find. Look on each sexual experience as an adventure with great potential for excitement and joy. Approach each time as if it were brand new. It is.

Since many survivors were deprived of the opportunity to go through the natural stages of sexual development, the survivor may find it helpful to go through an abbreviated repetition of missing stages with the participation or consent of the partner. These stages could include curiosity, homosexual variations, heterosexual exploration, flirting, first times, dating, promiscuity and going steady. Acting through a missing developmental stage gives the survivor an opportunity to grieve their loss and find a healing replacement experience.

Survivors of sexual abuse generally do not like surprises in the area of sex. The best results are usually obtained when the partner or survivor says what's going to happen next. Try narrating your foreplay. Move slowly so you can see or feel what you and your lover are going to do next. Say what you want to do and ask if your lover is ready. Consider what it would be like to hear a play-by-play description of the entire sexual experience.

Transference

Survivors sometimes react as if the partner were the perpetrator of their sexual abuse. Many partners at times report
feeling accused of being responsible for the abuse or in some
way identified with the abuser. This type of transference occurs most frequently in connection with sexual contact. It is
understandable that survivors might have lingering suspicions
regarding the motivation of anyone making sexual advances.

> Sometimes she recoils when I touch her like I was molesting
> her. I have to do things just right and I feel like I'm walking a
> tightrope. I have to be so careful that even I get a creepy feeling
> about our lovemaking. It seems like there are shadows of perpe-
> trators hovering overhead.

When transference occurs, the task for the survivor is to
separate partner from abuser, now from then, here from there.
The partner can assist in this task by saying, "I'm not your
abuser, no one is hurting you now, you are safe here." The
survivor learns in small steps that sex does not have to be
associated with memories of abuse.

Signs that transference is occurring are individual and depend on the survivor's abuse experience and defense mechanisms. They may include the survivor screaming, falling silent,
going limp or rigid, glazing over or other unlikely reactions.
It is best to stop any further sexual activity and re-establish
contact between partner and survivor. Ask, "What's going on?
Are you with me? What are you feeling?"

Often the partner and survivor can identify trigger behavior
that brings on a flashback. These behaviors may be specific
words, smells or kinds of touch that resemble the abuse
experience. Avoid sensitive trigger behavior as much as possible until the survivor is ready to try reclaiming the full
range of sexual behavior. This may mean taking an extra
bath or shower and using or not using a particular scent. This
is another area for constant communication and re-evaluation.
As an issue is resolved, an associated behavior may no longer

be taboo, or as additional memories surface, new trigger behavior may be identified.

When the survivor can usually remain present and enjoy the sex experience, it may be time to reclaim what has formerly been off limits. With the survivor's permission, the partner can lovingly try something that had to be avoided during early recovery. By cautious exploration and repetition, the survivor can expand the range of sexual behavior that is okay. The partner needs to respect the survivor's veto power and back off when asked. If not experiencing severe discomfort, the survivor may choose to push through the experience to confirm that nothing bad happens. The survivor may choose to tolerate something mildly unpleasant that the partner enjoys as a gift to the relationship. Sometimes pushing through minor discomfort is the fastest way for a survivor to acknowledge and work through a recurring issue.

Separation — Termination

Choosing to be in a relationship is a voluntary commitment for both partner and survivor. The emergence of sexual abuse issues is a trying experience that puts pressure on both and may result in separation or termination of the relationship. If the relationship has positive qualities, there may be some less extreme measures to be taken that can preserve it. Ultimately, each person must choose what is best.

Threatening separation over minor issues or at the first sign of trouble is not good problem-solving. Separation should not even come up in the discussion until the problem has been talked through many times and several negotiated solutions have been seriously tried and reluctantly discarded. If it appears that separation is inevitable, there are still options that may preserve the relationship or the possibility of a future relationship.

Redefining the relationship and the individual roles may make the problems manageable. Some partners and survivors have chosen to be celibate while remaining married or in a committed relationship. Not everyone can accept this option, but it becomes more possible after the sexual urgency of youth has passed and it may be preferable for those who have strong religious or personal reasons for staying together. Celibacy while in a relationship can be regarded as either a temporary and time-limited option or as a permanent solution.

Another possibility is to remain together while opening the relationship to outside sexual affairs. This may be no more than an overt recognition of what is already covertly taking place while affirming that the rest of the relationship is worth keeping. Recent statistics indicate that a large proportion of both women and men have had extramarital affairs. Again, religious or personal reasons may make this choice unacceptable, but there is no reason why society's expectations should rule out what the two individuals involved find workable.

Some partners and survivors have been successful in redefining a committed relationship into an intimate friendship with a lower level of commitment. This could be living as roommates rather than as a couple. It is hard to inch back from a relationship, and issues of betrayal and abandonment may surface when outside sex begins. Full discussion of all issues and expectations may make this option a possibility.

If there must be a separation, consider a temporary one. Things may improve enough during the period of separation so the problems can be resolved and the relationship resumed. If financing a temporary separation is a problem, try a temporary separation while living under the same roof. Separate bedrooms or sleeping on the couch might provide a cooling-off period. An extended vacation of a month or so or using a friend's guest room for a while could work out.

Marriage counseling may help before deciding to divorce or permanently terminate the relationship. An amicable separation is more likely if both parties have given their best toward resolving the problems and have negotiated in good faith for possible solutions. It is not healthy for either partner or survivor to remain deadlocked in a toxic relationship. A relationship that is seriously destructive to one or both may not be worth preserving.

I thought her therapy was going to fix the problems in our relationship, but it didn't turn out that way. The therapist saw problems coming and suggested some couples' sessions. So we went in and dragged out all the shit that we do to each other. At the end of the third couples' session she broke off the relationship. It hurt, and I'm filled with anger, sadness and loneliness.

I'm doing some writing about our relationship and the feelings it brought up. I can see now that it wasn't going to work, but I wanted to be the one to break it off. I've always been the first to leave in my other relationships. I don't have to stay in a relationship that's emotionally destructive. I have to take care of myself. I come first for me, and I can't fix her.

The decision to remain in a relationship with a survivor of sexual abuse is not easy, but there may be rewards that make it worthwhile. Partners who have stayed report being deeply moved by participating in the survivor's recovery and attaining greater levels of intimacy than any they had known before. Partners have also found that being in a relationship with a survivor requires a commitment to self-awareness and honesty that is highly conducive to their own personal growth. Partners who remain with survivors should know that they do so voluntarily in the belief that the rewards outweigh the costs.

Ongoing Abuse

Some survivors seem to have a need to place themselves in situations similar or comparable to the original sexual abuse situation. This may include voluntarily placing themselves in subservient or degrading roles relative to the partner and insisting that the partner is doing them a service by complying with their requests. This repetition compulsion of survivors may reflect the fact that sexual abuse is the only kind of sexual experience they have had and is the only way they know how to be sexual. Some other survivors reconstruct sexually abusive situations using role reversal with themselves in the dominant, controlling or powerful position. Again, this repeats the kind of sexual behavior they have learned.

Rather than complying with the survivor's invitation, partners are urged to avoid activity that is in any way sexually

abusive and to insist on developing a more healthy and functional sexual relationship. This means avoiding sado-maso-
chism or bondage and discipline with survivors. Two healthy
individuals are free to voluntarily participate in any kind of
sexual activity they want, but it is counterproductive for survivors to be involved in the repetition of sexually abusive
situations. It keeps them stuck in trying to do the abuse over
and do it right so it concludes with better results. This is an
impossible task, since the sexual abuse should never have
happened and doing it over cannot have a beneficial outcome.

Survivors often choose relationships that are physically or
emotionally abusive. Many sexual abuse survivors are also
victims of spouse abuse or physical battery. Although it may
not be a conscious choice, survivors often find themselves in
abusive relationships because they are familiar. The survivors'
defense mechanisms allow them to feel comfortable in dan-
gerous situations. Low self-esteem is also a contributing factor,
since many survivors subconsciously believe they do not deserve to be treated any better.

Partners who see the survivor entering abusive relationships
again and again, on the job or in social situations, can objec-
tively describe what they see. The goal is to build the survivor's
self-esteem to the point where abusive relationships can be
broken off and avoided in the future.

Linda's mother was an alcoholic and her father was the "perp."
She used to do all kinds of things for her father and I let her do
the same things for me. She wanted to do it, and I used to think
it was okay even though I had a funny feeling about it at the time.
Now I see that I was being sexually abusive and I feel a lot of
shame about it. This is hard to talk about, and it's hard to admit
that I hurt her too. It wasn't intentional; I thought I was pleasing
her. I feel like I was set up and in some ways I'm a victim too.

My mother let everyone in the family walk all over her and I
thought that was okay too. I'm beginning to have better boundaries so I don't unintentionally exploit other people. I'm learning to control my impulses; I don't have to act on every one. If
I feel the slightest hesitancy, it's better to do nothing until I'm
sure. Sooner or later I'll know for sure whether it's a boundary

violation or not. I know that the more I want to do something, the easier it is to fool myself. But if I go ahead and do it and I'm wrong, I'll be sorry later. At least I'm not walking blindly into boundary issues any more without some warning of what I'm doing.

If you recognize yourself as a partner having a role in perpetuating the abuse of the survivor, take action to stop it for your own sake. Abusive partners are emotionally sick themselves and need to seek professional help. If you are aware of your role, you have probably already recognized that it is wrong and have honestly tried to stop. Somehow it keeps happening even though you have promised yourself never to do it again. Feeling sorry and miserable after a destructive outburst won't result in a permanent change.

Change is possible, but only with outside help. If you need help or know someone who does, call the county welfare department or mental health agency and find out what resources are available in the area. Many are free or have a sliding scale based on income. Whatever the problem, it can be fixed. There is no situation too difficult to be improved. You are not alone, and there is someone who can help you. Do it for the survivor who has already been damaged enough, and do it for yourself.

6

Understanding
A Survivor

Since survivors can be of any age, sex, race or economic group and since the effects of the sexual abuse can range from mild to severe, it's hard to give any descriptions that will apply to all survivors. However, sexual abuse has a distinct impact that can often be recognized before the survivor has any memory of the experience. Childhood sexual abuse usually results in more noticeable and pronounced effects and behavior patterns. Survivors who have established an adult life before the abuse occurred are likely to show fewer of these effects and in milder form. Once these patterns become apparent, however, it is hard to understand why they weren't noticed long ago.

On the surface survivors often appear to be doing fine, but it doesn't take much probing to find out that something is missing. For a survivor, coping with life may be described as looking good on the outside while making do and feeling miserable on the inside. Survivors live with a constant state of numbness in which nothing seems to matter or to be completely real. Their approach to problem-solving is to hope the problem will go away if they just don't think about it.

Survivors usually have well-developed defense mechanisms that mask the existence of the effects of sexual abuse. Among these are denial and minimization, the hallmarks of sexual abuse survivors. They deny the frequency, duration, severity and even the existence of the sexual abuse. If aware of it, they minimize its effects, insisting it wasn't that bad or it didn't really affect them. Survivors may persist in this self-delusion even in the presence of incontrovertible evidence of the serious and long-standing effects sexual abuse has had on their lives. The proof is in their dysfunctional adult behavior patterns.

Several common behavioral characteristics are frequently observed in survivors. These behaviors are so common that the presence of a significant number of them is highly indicative of childhood sexual abuse. Many of these behaviors are puzzling and don't seem to make sense to partners or maybe not to the survivors themselves. Yet if a behavior didn't make sense on some level, we wouldn't do it. There has to be a reason for behavior that is repeated or sustained. We don't do things over and over without cause. So even though it may not seem rational, there is usually a reason on a deeper level, rooted in the sexual abuse experience, which explains these puzzling behaviors.

The descriptions of the characteristic behaviors of survivors offer some possible explanations of why they do make sense. In most cases they were necessary skills that enabled the survivor to cope with the sexual abuse experience or with its effects. They may in fact have been the only way to survive the experience. While these characteristic behaviors were at one time highly functional ways to survive extreme circumstances, they no longer serve the survivor. The survivor's task is to translate these no longer functional behaviors into something that makes better sense. Why is this behavior the best idea the survivor can come up with at the moment? Are there any better ideas that are more appropriate for the present circumstances? Partners who understand can remind survivors of these questions and may be able to enhance their recovery.

Victim Role

The survivors of sexual abuse are often found in situations in which they are likely to be victims of repeated physical, emotional or sexual abuse. It is not uncommon for a survivor to be the victim of violent crime or some other fraudulent, abusive or exploitive action. If not misused by someone else, survivors often cause their own problems by failing to take care of themselves properly or by being excessively accident-prone.

Having been victimized by the sexual abuse experience, a survivor is likely to internalize this role and unconsciously act in ways that invite victimization. Having been treated with disrespect, survivors have come to disrespect themselves and believe they deserve nothing better. The internal expectation of being a victim becomes a self-fulfilling prophecy. Survivors need to learn to say no and to practice saying "No," beginning with small and insignificant things. Survivors who can't say "No" need to begin literally by learning to form the word with their mouths. Partners can allow, encourage and respect the survivor's growing assertiveness. The survivor's task is to stop accepting the victim role and to start living with vitality, claiming victory over past circumstances. By holding onto an image of the survivor as a strong and capable person, the partner can assist in leaving the victim role behind.

Occluded Memory

Having no memory of childhood sexual abuse is perhaps the most common characteristic of survivors of childhood sexual abuse. Anyone who has no recollection of large periods of childhood is certainly repressing the memory of a traumatic and painful time that often includes sexual abuse. This single characteristic, with the addition of any other bit of evidence, can usually be considered diagnostic of childhood sexual abuse.

Childhood sexual abuse is so traumatic and stressful that no child could be expected to cope with it alone. Blocking conscious awareness and denying that it occurred is the coping strategy that allows the child to survive. Once the immediate safety of the survivor is assured, the blocked memories will come up in one way or another and demand attention. The survivor must reckon with the memories as they surface — in a flood, in flashbacks, in unexplained tears, in special sensitivity or in gut-level feelings.

Body Memory

Body memory is a term that describes recurring sensory feelings of something beyond the immediate situation. A particular sight, smell or touch may cause a survivor to have a profoundly uneasy feeling. Some survivors describe unpleasant feelings sweeping over their genitals at unexpected moments when no one else is present and no one is touching them. It's as if the body had a memory of its own that is expressed by a recurrence of the sensation without a corresponding awareness of its cause.

Athletes repeat the same movements over and over to train their bodies to react in a particular manner under particular circumstances without conscious intervention. The sexual abuse experience has had a similar effect on the body of the survivor. Repressed body memories resurface just as mental ones do. Survivors should accept that body memories do not mean they are crazy. Instead, body memories should be given the same recognition and attention as cognitive memories during the process of recovery.

Triggers

Triggers are specific touches, sights, sounds or smells that evoke a memory or other legacies of the sexual abuse experience, usually against the wishes of the survivor. Triggers are usually associated with unwanted consequences like shame attacks and recurrences of dissociation or other survival mechanisms. Survivors usually take conscious or unconscious steps to protect themselves from their triggers.

The necessity to avoid triggers means survivors are limited in the range of activity they may participate in safely. One of the goals of recovery is to defuse the triggers by gradually reducing the severity of the reaction until the survivor experiences it only as a mild discomfort or not at all. The partner can support the survivor by avoiding triggers until the survivor is ready to press through the attenuated negative response. Eliminating triggers enables the survivor to reclaim the full range of choices in life.

It's not possible to avoid triggers at all times, and it's also not desirable. Learning new responses for triggers is part of the survivor's recovery process. Each time something triggers flashback memories, dissociation or other defense mechanisms provide another opportunity to partially defuse that trigger. Survivors may need reassurance to talk themselves through the experience using self-talk like: "It's in the past." "You can handle it; you're an adult now." "The memory is no worse than what you've already been through." It's important for the survivor to avoid using alcohol, drugs or other acting-out behavior that could interfere with staying present through the experience.

After the incident the survivor may need the partner's support to interpret the experience and process the feelings. Questions to ask include: "What was the trigger?" "What were you afraid of?" "What emotions came up?" "When have these same emotions come up before?" "What did the experience remind you of?" "What are you able to do for yourself now that you weren't able to do before?" "What options do you have to handle the situation differently the next time?"

After processing, expect a reaction that leaves the survivor feeling unprotected and vulnerable. Allow time and space to rest and get comfort. As part of the process of learning healthier behavior, the survivor will need to talk about the experience with friends, in support groups and in therapy. Repeatedly describing the incident and what was learned is a method of mental rehearsal that enables the survivor to defuse the trigger.

Sexual Preference

Statistics show approximately 60 percent of the population of both sexes are exclusively heterosexual and approximately

10 percent are exclusively homosexual. This leaves approximately 30 percent who are bisexual or who experience some confusion about their sexual identity and sexual preference. A large proportion of these 30 percent have been victims of childhood sexual abuse. While recovery from sexual abuse would have little effect on the sexual preference of those who are clearly heterosexual or clearly homosexual, recovery may resolve the confusion for those who fall within the 30 percent.

Since human sexuality is not instinctual and there are some commonly accepted developmental stages during which sexual behavior is learned, it is not surprising that childhood sexual abuse could have some effect on a person's sexuality and sexual preference. The effect varies from person to person. It depends on the length of time and age during which the sexual abuse occurred and the developmental steps the individual completed before or after the abuse experience.

Although there are many theories regarding sexual development, the common stages for heterosexual development begin with the pre-erotic period of infancy. We discover and explore our own sexual organs during early childhood and through curiosity compare genitals first with members of the same sex and then the opposite sex. During the prepuberty period, the opposite sex is regarded with suspicion or disgust. There is usually some experimental erotic contact (mutual masturbation) with other members of the same sex which is still largely self-focused. During and after puberty interest turns toward the opposite sex, and sexuality becomes a shared activity between two individuals who are focused on each other. Homosexual developmental stages are similar, except there is usually an exploratory period with the opposite sex after puberty before interest returns to members of the same sex.

Survivors whose sexual development was interrupted by the intrusion of childhood sexual abuse may need to repeat or re-explore any missing or deficient developmental stages. Partners can support this by talking about what it was like for them and allowing the survivor to grieve the loss of not having a comparable life experience. This can also help unlock the survivor's anger at the perpetrator. The task for survivors is to complete any unresolved developmental stages and clarify any uncertainty about their sexual identity or sexual preference. The goal is for survivors to feel satisfied and comfortable with their choice of lifestyle and come to peace with their expressed sexual preference.

Psychosomatic/Recurring Illnesses

Survivors frequently have psychosomatic or recurring illnesses that are related to their sexual abuse experiences. For example, survivors forced to perform oral sex may have frequent throat infections. Other related illnesses can include frequent vaginal or urinary infections and bowel or bladder problems. Some survivors experience paralysis or weakness of extremities or body parts that were immobilized during the abuse. Also commonly reported are asthma and many varieties of allergic reactions. In some cases an organic cause for the illness can be found; in other cases the illness appears to be psychosomatic. Certainly the mind can have an effect on the body and sexual abuse can have a profound effect upon the mind.

Partners and survivors can observe the survivor's health records and notice any patterns that begin to emerge. Frequent illness can be a source of additional information that can be acknowledged and used during the recovery process. This is a highly individual area and may not be related in every case. Some survivors in recovery have noted a decreasing frequency in such illnesses and an improvement in overall health.

Self-Mutilation

One troubling behavior that is hard for both partners and survivors to understand is self-mutilation. A surprising number of survivors engage in behavior that is painful or disfiguring to themselves. Cuts and burns are perhaps the most frequently reported. Milder forms include compulsively cutting hair, pulling out eyebrows or patches of hair, picking at skin blemishes, biting finger nails or cuticles, piercing other than earlobes and using bizarre makeup styles. Getting a tattoo, especially self-tattooing, may in some cases be regarded as self-mutilation.

Survivors may not initially be able to recognize or acknowledge such acts as self-mutilation. Once aware that they are destructive and undesired behaviors, the survivor may not be able to stop their recurrence. If survivors have been hurt by sexual abuse, how can it make sense to be causing themselves greater pain? One reason may be that the survivor has no words to express the inner pain. For sexual abuse inflicted at an early age on survivors who were preverbal or had limited vocabularies, self-mutilation may be the only way to show what they cannot tell.

The inner pain and depression associated with sexual abuse is chronic and unrelenting. There is no way for the survivor to find even temporary relief from this inner turmoil, and in the early stages every memory may intensify the pain to critical proportions. Choosing to inflict a more immediate and excruciating level of pain from a cut or burn can temporarily give the survivor control by diverting attention away from the deeper sexual abuse issues from which there seems to be no way to attain relief.

After a few moments of stabbing or throbbing pain, the brain releases endorphins that function like a narcotic to decrease the level of pain. The endorphins also reduce the overall level of anxiety and consequently provide some relief from the inner pain and turmoil. Self-inflicted physical pain paradoxically acts to relieve mental agony and anguish. Survivors wouldn't do it if it didn't work.

Scratching, biting or picking at oneself can also be seen as an attempt to get at the unseen inner wounds from the sexual abuse. The visibility of a self-inflicted tattoo or the flow of blood from a cut is an attempt to externalize the internal pain. Self-mutilation represents an unsuccessful attempt to bring effects of sexual abuse out into the open so they can be seen. Survivors learned in childhood that physical injuries get noticed while emotional pain is ignored.

The survivor's task is to look for other ways to express inner pain and turmoil and find other ways to experience relief. What would the feeling be if there were words to express it? What can I do with the pain? How else can that need be filled? Some survivors find that receiving hugs and nurturing touch makes the urge to self-mutilate go away. The partner can say in actions and words, "You don't have to cut yourself to show me your pain."

Suicide Attempts

Survivors in crisis, usually during the initial flood of memories, may feel overwhelmed by their feelings and see no way out other than suicide. Continuing and unrelenting inner pain may also cause some survivors to consider suicide as a way out. Most suicide attempts are desperate cries for help, and getting that help is the essential response.

Most people who are honest with themselves can recall a time of emotional turmoil, possibly during teenage years, when they had idle thoughts of suicide. These thoughts occurred in response to some stressful or traumatic experience, and except for lingering feelings of shame they usually disappeared as fast as they came. They may have been coupled with thoughts like "Boy, wouldn't they be sorry if I were really dead?" Various plans and options are considered only briefly and there is usually no real intention of carrying them out. Survivors need to release the shame about fleeting thoughts of suicide by acknowledging them to their partners and support groups.

Transient thoughts of suicide, a symptom of mild distress, are usually resolved when the underlying stressful situation is resolved. However, suicidal thoughts must be treated more seriously if they are prolonged, occur frequently or go beyond vague plans. Is there a well-thought-out plan with a specific method, time and place? Have there been any preparations through obtaining necessary information, materials or equipment? Has there been any disposition or giving away of possessions and pets? Has a will or suicide note been prepared? Has there been a dry run or partial carrying out of the plan? Have there been previous suicide attempts?

There's no time to waste if things have advanced to the point that suicide seems to be a positive solution for taking charge of a desperate and hopeless situation. When this up-side-down logic sets in, there is a danger that the suicide plan may be carried out. This kind of confused thinking can result in accidental or unintentional suicide if help is not obtained immediately.

Partners must not feel they are the only source of help. Take seriously any talk of suicidal thoughts; call the suicide prevention hotline and get other appropriate professional assistance. The partner can keep the survivor talking until the survivor comes to agree that suicide is not an option. Feeling suicidal is just a feeling, no matter how painful or intense. If not acted out, suicidal feelings will change into a more hopeful emotional state. Suicide really doesn't resolve anything. It is a permanent and irreversible conclusion for a temporary problem. The survivor's feelings of crisis will pass. Recovery isn't easy but many have found relief and serenity. Healing from the effects of sexual abuse can become a reality for every survivor.

Dissociation/Splitting Off

Dissociation or splitting off is one of the most common coping mechanisms used by sexual abuse survivors. Those who were forced to undergo intensely distasteful sexual abuse usually find the experience too much to bear. Since the survivor is prevented from physically leaving, the only remaining option is mental escape. This process of separating or splitting off inner thought and awareness from the normal flow of incoming sensory experience is called dissociation.

Survivors whose behavior during dissociation is noticeably different often describe the experience as splitting or splitting off. Usually this does not mean the survivor is psychotic or has a split personality. An extreme psychiatric diagnosis of this sort is comparatively rare among survivors, as is the occurrence of multiple personality disorder. Most of us experience some variability in our personality — for example, adopting a conservative business style at work and a more unrestrained lifestyle on the weekend. The person is aware of each style of behavior and when the switches back and forth occur. Survivors too are usually aware of how their behavior changes after splitting off and when the changes occur. With true multiple personality disorder, each personality is convinced it is the only one. Each is only dimly aware of the possible existence of other personalities, except for a record-keeping personality whose function is to have complete memory and full awareness of all alternate personalities. Usually each personality has almost no memory of any other existence.

Survivors usually have milder forms of splitting off that are triggered by recognizable recollections or situations and end when the memory fades or the situation again becomes safe. Survivors know when they are fully aware and when they are partially or fully split off from what is going on in the present. Splitting off resembles multiple personality disorder and may respond to similar treatment methods. Descriptions of individuals with multiple personalities may also be helpful for survivors who are trying to understand and make sense of their own behavior. Survivors who discover someone else's clothes unexplainably appearing in their closets or who experience blocks of lost time in their current lives may actually be suffering from a multiple personality disorder. This relatively rare diagnosis is more common among survivors of prolonged, severe and ritual sexual abuse.

I'm the partner of an incest survivor and I've got kind of a unique problem. My survivor's a multiple, and I need to talk to somebody to figure out how to handle it. Sometimes I think I'm the one who's going crazy. I think I'm talking to her, and then I find out I've been talking to one of six other people who look just like her. We talk about an issue, let's say money, and I think we've got a deal about how much we're going to spend. Then she flips into another personality and the deal's off. Her spendthrift personality buys a CD player and a half a dozen CDs. She doesn't remember that we talked about our budget or that we even had a conversation. The next day she's back, accusing me of going over-budget for lunch by $1.50 with no awareness that she's already blown the budget by hundreds of dollars.

I'm getting a little smarter than I used to be, though. I'm beginning to pick up on the little cues so I can figure out whether

I'm talking to the real Susie or one of her other selves. I recognize that her other selves aren't integrated with her real self and aren't as far along in recovery. I love her a lot and I can't really get angry with her, if I can even figure out who to get angry at. All I can do is tell her what I see and let her use the information to increase her own awareness and reintegrate her multiple personalities.

Splitting off and dissociation occur spontaneously in response to severely stressful or traumatic experiences to protect the survivor from being overwhelmed. For survivors, dissociation or splitting off from present situations is often an automatic reaction. It parallels the dissociation response that originally occurred during the sexual abuse experience. The degree of dissociation that survivors experience in current situations varies from "going numb" in portions of their bodies, to leaving the body and observing from outside, to completely "checking out." The degree of dissociation is usually proportional to the level of danger or potential threat.

The protective response of dissociation no longer serves the survivor if it automatically occurs when it is not needed or if it prevents the survivor from being present during desired experiences. The partner can assist the survivor in decreasing the degree of dissociation and the automatic nature of the response by noticing when it occurs. Call the survivor back by asking, "Where are you? Are you with me now? What made you go?"

Hostage Syndrome

The hostage syndrome describes a reaction induced by stress or terror in which victims who have been taken hostage develop an emotional bond and a sense of allegiance with their captors. This syndrome is common when the hostages perceive rejection and lack of expected support during and after their victimization, especially if negotiations for their release are delayed and prolonged. The hostage syndrome also describes the victims' behavior after the incident is over, when they may embrace their captors and plead for lenient treatment.

Survivors of sexual abuse, like hostages, may form an emotional bond with their abusers. This attachment may mean the survivor keeps the abuse secret out of loyalty to the abuser and protectively springs to the abuser's defense. It is not uncommon for survivors of childhood sexual abuse to show a greater degree of attachment to the abusive parent than to the nonabusive parent. These survivors also find it easier to become enraged at the nonabusive parent for failing to provide adequate protection than at the abusive parent for committing the abusive acts.

Survivors need to know these are natural reactions to the devastating effects of the sexual abuse in which their sense of self-esteem and independence was destroyed, they were not given appropriate protection and they were forced to rely on their abusers. Some survivors may even have deluded themselves into believing their abusers were truly concerned and had their best interests at heart. Survivors need to forgive themselves for any sense of guilt or self-blame that remains, keeping the sympathy for themselves instead of the abuser.

Partners can assist survivors by maintaining a consistent view of the abusive experience with responsibility for the abuse placed squarely on the abuser. The survivor is not to blame for the situation and is not to blame for developing an attachment to the abuser. This, like other survival skills, was necessary for the survivor to live through the experience. Sympathize with the survivor, not with the abuser. Survivors have difficulty enough feeling sympathy for themselves and need reinforcement for this difficult task. There is not enough sympathy available at this stage to meet the survivor's needs and have any left over for the abuser. Sympathy for the abuser comes much later, if at all.

Fantasies And Dreams

Some survivors report having recurring fantasies or dreams of being raped or taking a role in sexually abusive situations. The survivor has no conscious desire to be sexually abused, but the fantasies or dreams keep happening. Usually they are involuntary and are frightening to the survivor. Some survivors, however, experience fantasies of being forced or overpowered as pleasurable and this may be the only way they can reach orgasm.

Survivors' fantasies or dreams of being sexually abused do not mean they want to be sexually abused again, and the fantasies do not have to be acted out. Survivors who can only experience orgasm through the use of such fantasies have been affected by their sexual abuse experience to such an extent that their sexual response is conditioned on a fantasy repetition of the abuse.

Fantasies and dreams may be ways for unconscious issues to emerge and may be used in the recovery process to uncover and heal past abusive experiences. Fantasies can be controlled and used by the survivor as a mental rehearsal of a desirable response or different kind of behavior. For example, the fantasy can be played back with the power roles reversed, with the intervention of the adult survivor as a super hero, with a different outcome or with a transformation into a more functional way of being. We do not have to be the victims of our fantasies and dreams; instead, we can use them to our own advantage. Sharing and discussing fantasies and dreams with partners or counselors might provide some insight. This may result in the survivor getting ideas or directed imagery of more functional behavior to use in fantasy and dream.

Repetition

With surprising frequency, survivors place themselves in situations where they are repeatedly victims of sexual abuse or some other type of physical, mental or emotional abuse. This may occur because it is a repetition of what the survivors have been taught and is the only way of relating they know. Survivors may have internalized as part of their own identity that their only value was as a sex object or for the sexual service they could perform. The repetition compulsion goes along with low self-esteem and the inner belief that the survivor does not deserve to be treated any better. A low sense of self-worth results in the survivor's distorted view that being abused is what it means to be loved.

Survivors are usually unaware that they are setting up this type of relationship until it's too late. The familiarity and intensity of being involved with a powerful partner are so attractive that the survivor does it again and again. It's as if on some level the survivor is attempting to relive the abusive situation and this time do it right. But being abused is never okay and there is no way to do it right.

The repetition compulsion continues until there is some awareness of the process and desire to avoid it in the future. New behavior patterns must be based on the survivor and partner sharing power and control rather than the survivor giving up all power and control to the partner. Abstinence for survivors of sexual abuse means getting out and staying out of abusive relationships.

Re-enactment

Re-enactment means passing it on to the next generation. Many survivors recreate the behavior patterns from their families of origin that gave rise to the sexual abuse. This happens in spite of the fact that most survivors have sworn they would not do what their parents have done. Even if the same type of abuse is consciously avoided, the abuse may be passed on to the survivor's children in a different way. It may show up as physical, mental or emotional abuse. Survivors who have not recovered a full sense of self and what it means to be loved themselves will pass on a defective view of love to their children.

Survivors know what it is like to have no power and control, and having gained power and control they are not about to relinquish a bit of it. Some survivors have heard, "I can discipline you because I am the parent, and when you are the parent, you will have your turn." As a result, some survivors are afraid to discipline their children for fear they will not be able to control themselves or to stop once they have started. Since survivors often have an unclear perception of boundaries, their parenting styles and methods of discipline may abusively violate the boundaries of their children.

Many survivors doubt their ability to be good parents and are afraid they are going to be abusive in some way. Most child abusers were themselves abused as children, so survivors are definitely at risk of being abusive. This is a difficult issue to face since most survivors have such strong negative feelings toward child abusers. It is typical for a survivor to say something like, "The thought of me abusing my own children is so horrible that I can't think about it." Suppression of negative thoughts makes it more likely that they will emerge unconsciously and against our will. We can only do what we were taught, and it is better to face our dark side rather than being surprised when a negative impulse emerges.

Although statistics show that many of those who abuse their children were also abused by their parents, there is absolutely no evidence indicating it is genetically linked. This means survivors can definitely break the cycle and triumph over their upbringing by consciously changing the parenting and discipline styles acquired from their parents. Re-education is possible. We can learn better options than raising a hand in anger or physically, mentally, emotionally or sexually abusing our children. Partner and survivor alike can attend parenting classes and get the resources necessary to be cycle-breakers who do not re-enact the abuse and pass it on.

Low Sex Drive/Easily Stimulated

Survivors usually find that their sexuality is out of balance in one of two ways. Either their sexuality is in the deep freeze or it is in overdrive. Partners of survivors whose sexuality is in the deep freeze wonder if they will ever have a regular sex life again, and partners of survivors whose sexuality is in overdrive wonder if such frequent sex can have any meaning.

Survivors with low or nonexistent sex drives often report feelings of revulsion about specific sex acts, the opposite sex, the perpetrator's sex or the perpetrator's age group. The survivor's feelings are not specifically directed at the partner. The survivor's sexual abuse experience causes an involuntary emotional response to sexuality in any form. This broad-brush approach allows the survivor to feel safe, but also prevents any experience of sexual intimacy. A variation of this occurs when the survivor only feels like having sex when the partner is at work, out of town, or when other circumstances make actual sexual intercourse impossible. Only when sex is impossible does the survivor feel safe enough to allow sexual feelings to flow.

The task for the low sex drive survivor is to separate the partner from the feelings of revulsion rightfully directed at the perpetrator. Only the perpetrator committed the act of sexual abuse. It was not done by all members of the same sex and particularly not the partner. It may be helpful for the partner to stop using specific behavior that the survivor most closely associates with the perpetrator or the sexual abuse.

Survivors who are easily stimulated may have been conditioned by the sexual abuse experience to regard themselves as sex objects. This becomes internalized and incorporated as part of the survivor's sense of identity. Being sexual is an automatic response and may be the only way easily stimulated survivors have of being intimate and sharing who they are. Lack of responsiveness from the partner may be experienced as rejection, abandonment or loss of love. The survivor only feels self-worth and value when performing sexual service which the partner accepts as proof of love.

Survivors who seek constant sex need to find other ways of expressing love and feeling valued in the relationship. The partner can assist by frequently recognizing and validating all of the survivor's good qualities in addition to sexuality. Find ways to build on an identity and lifestyle that does not depend exclusively on sexuality.

Promiscuity

Some survivors find themselves acting out sexually and engaging in promiscuous behavior, often against their will. These contacts usually have a driven quality and are not completely enjoyable. If pleasurable, they are somewhat less than satisfying and are not lasting. For some survivors this is turning the table on the perpetrator. They were used in the sexual abuse experience; now they are getting back by using others. In some cases this leads survivors into extreme behavior such as group sex, swinging or prostitution. The ability to numb out and dissociate from their bodies allows sexual abuse survivors to endure degrading sex acts without complaint.

Promiscuity can also be seen as a way of acting out the repetition compulsion. Survivors may act out because this is the only way they were able to receive attention in their families. Being abused was better than receiving no attention at all. Human beings need to be touched, and survivors will seek out the same kind of situations that successfully resulted in being touched. Promiscuity, like sexual abuse, may be perceived as nurturing touch if it is the only kind of touch the survivor knows. The abuse experience may also have led the survivor to believe their only value was for the sexual service they could perform.

Abstinence from promiscuity and sexual acting out is usually necessary for survivors to recover. Since sex is a basic drive, total sexual abstinence is usually not successful in the long term. Survivors who are learning the difference between healthy sexual experiences and dysfunctional promiscuity or acting out may have some slips or make some misjudgments. The partner needs to understand that the survivor's promiscuity is a reaction from the sexual abuse experience. It is not directed at the partner, even though it may be hurtful to the partner. Partners can choose to express their hurt in a way that recognizes the perpetrator rather than the survivor as ultimately being responsible.

Sex And Love Addiction

Survivors may recognize in themselves repetition of behavior that meets the definition of sex and love addiction. This may include promiscuity, repeated love affairs, romanticized relationships, multiple concurrent relationships, a series of short-term relationships or a compulsive need for frequent sexual behavior of any type. Many sex and love addicts describe an inability to stop pursuing masturbation or other sexual activity to the point of exhaustion, pain or injury. The common characteristic is that sex and love addiction is a pattern of compulsive and mood-altering behavior that is harmful to the survivor and others. It is a way of avoiding feelings and dealing with the issues of recovery from sexual abuse.

Having experienced the overwhelming intensity of incest or sexual abuse, the survivor feels compelled to rediscover and re-experience that intensity. Survivors engage in this type of behavior to seek out the excitement and intensity of new love and first sexual experiences. Sex and love addicts love falling in love and the experience of merging with another person. They are in love, not with the other person, but with the way it makes them feel. Once the newness of the experience is over, the relationship is over. There is a continuing drive to repeat the romantic experience and to find ever more exciting ways of behavior in spite of the consequences.

Sex and love addiction is like other addictions and can be understood in the same ways. Relationships are the addictive substance and the cause of euphoria, habituation, protecting the supply, disease, depression and death. Instead of allowing the initial passion to form the basis of a long-term committed relationship, sex and love addicts are driven to experience initial passion again and again. It is a misguided attempt to feel okay about oneself by looking for outside solutions for an inside problem. Intense relationships and experiences may provide momentary relief from the depression and pain of a shame-based identity, but they do not deal with the sexual abuse that is the root of the problem. Abstinence from addictive behavior in this area is also necessary for survivor's recovery. As with recovery from promiscuity, survivors may have slips as they learn to form healthy sex and love relationships. Again, wise partners recognize that the behaviors associated with sex and love addiction are not directed at the partner.

Low Self-Esteem

Sexual abuse is an experience that shatters self-esteem. Most survivors struggle through life with a low sense of self-esteem. Since the sexual self is close to the core of our being, sexual abuse is experienced as a violation of the special and unique qualities that are the foundation of our self-esteem. Whatever resistance the survivor was able to offer was overpowered and the survivor was forced to succumb to an uncontrollable power. The survivor, abandoned to face the abuser alone, felt betrayed by those who should have provided protection. Through this personal experience with the irrational and incomprehensible, the survivor lost faith in role models. With hope and trust destroyed, the survivor lacks the self-esteem necessary to risk the self-exposure and vulnerability necessary to heal.

Reclaiming self-esteem is something survivors need to do side-by-side with other recovery tasks. This is done by rebuilding the foundations of self-esteem that were broken by the sexual abuse experience. Find the uniqueness that is the core of self-esteem and protect it with functional boundaries that expand as self-esteem grows. Discover the parts of the self that can be controlled and become empowered to change them. Re-establish connectedness with those who are able to offer support. Ask for directions from a mentor who has experience and a guide who can offer hope. Rebuild the shattered trust needed to risk incremental steps to recovery and personal growth.

Survivors and partners can elevate their self-esteem together, each supporting the other's growth. One of the hallmarks of high self-esteem is that when we feel good about ourselves, we have plenty to share.

Poor Self-Image

Survivors often have a poor self-image that is out of conformity with reality. Survivors often fail to recognize or fully value their own accomplishments. Having been devalued by the sexual abuse experience, they now discount and devalue themselves. To avoid attracting positive attention, they may be careless about their grooming and hygiene, wear little or no make-up, and have drab and uninteresting wardrobes. They feel unworthy of praise and undeserving of compliments. Survivors are quick to credit others rather than graciously accepting public recognition and acknowledgment.

The goal for survivors is to gain a true and accurate self-image that clearly recognizes the positive without undue emphasis on the negative. Partners can support this by serving as objective observers of the survivor's reality, describing successes with truth and accuracy. Since survivors are often their own worst critics and have already overdone self-criticism, it is usually not helpful for partners to offer even the best-intentioned constructive criticism.

Body-Shy

Observers of sexual abuse survivors often notice physical tenseness, rigidity and awkwardness, qualities that show survivors' lack of comfort in their bodies. Survivors often slump and take on a guarded posture that is not fluid and mobile. Survivors' circulation may be suppressed, causing them to be easily chilled and their skin to feel cold. Survivors are generally clumsy and lack physical agility. Many dread exercise and do not experience pleasure in movement. They think they can't dance, avoid active sports, and dislike strenuous physical activity. In physical competition, they fail to excel and stop short of an all-out effort. Body-shy is a term used to describe survivors' characteristic lack of ease and grace in the movement of their bodies.

Survivors in recovery are encouraged to learn to take full possession of their bodies and to comport themselves with confidence. Some survivors have been helped by massage or various types of body movement therapy. This is most successful in conjunction with counseling to deal with the inevitable release of feelings that comes with reintegration of physical mobility. Partners can be supportive by applauding the survivor's participation in even the most sedentary sport. Try taking an exercise class or dance class together. Invite the survivor to join in a safe physical activity and offer steady encouragement. A little persistence with body-shy survivors is okay if a truly safe activity has been chosen.

Body Armor And Emaciation

Although many people are overweight as a result of the common American diet and lifestyle, a large number of survivors are found among the significantly overweight and obese. It's as if layers of fat have been added as a protection against unwanted physical touch. Survivors are generally unsuccessful in dieting and weight reduction programs or quickly regain any lost weight because they feel too vulnerable without the body armor. For long-term success, survivors must also address the issues of sexual abuse.

An alternative adaptive mechanism used by survivors is anorexia to the point of emaciation. This can result in suppressing the development of secondary sexual characteristics. Anorexic survivors of both sexes may almost look more like children than adults. They try to avoid the sexual abuse issues by presenting a nonsexual appearance. Anorexic survivors are on some level afraid that filling out may invite unwanted sexual advances.

Part of the problem is that survivors were not taught good self-care in their dysfunctional families and do not know how to feed themselves properly. Nutritional education helps, but a healthy diet is not the total solution. There is sometimes a misguided tendency to focus on weight as the solution for eating disorders, with overeaters trying to bring their weight down and anorexics trying to bring their weight up. From this perspective, the eating disorder would be solved if only the survivor could maintain normal weight through health club membership and dieting or exercising. In fact, eating disorders — like alcoholism — cannot be cured by willpower alone. Survivors with eating disorders are not to blame for having an additional disease. They need the help of therapy, counseling or a treatment program in order to recover from it.

Survivors with dual identification of both sexual abuse and eating disorders need to pursue programs for both problems. Sympathetic partners can be supportive of both programs with the knowledge that they reinforce each other. Sometimes progress in one program occurs at the same time as relapse in the other program, while at other times relapse occurs simultaneously. Long-term recovery will require success in both programs.

Excessive Clothing

Survivors often wear excessive clothing inappropriate for the weather conditions — a coat or jacket indoors or multiple layers even in warm weather. The clothing may also be an attempt to conceal an overweight or underweight condition. Discomfort with body appearance may result in the survivor always wearing long sleeves and long pants. In the bedroom survivors may insist on lights out and refuse to wear anything but completely covering bed clothes. The survivor may be unwilling to go swimming or participate in sports that expose the extremities. Many survivors seem to need at least one layer of clothing to protect their bodies from visibility and unwanted touch.

The task for survivors is to become comfortable within their bodies so it is no longer necessary to wear excessive clothing. Survivors also need to learn how to use physical and emotional boundaries so they can be protected without constantly carrying an uncomfortable barrier of fabric. Encouraging partners can discuss in advance what kind of dress might be appropriate for upcoming activities, events and circumstances. Practice with using and respecting boundaries also helps alleviate the necessity for protective clothing.

Overcompensation

If sexual abuse is so devastating, what explains the fact that some survivors are well-organized, highly successful and seem to show no effects from the sexual abuse? Some survivors seem to have every aspect of their lives organized with everything in its place and "to do" lists that get done on time. They may have established successful careers in which they are recognized for their achievements and hard work. Their lives seem to be under control. This is likely to be an overcompensation for the lack of control the survivor feels on the inside. Survivors are often driven to excel to compensate for inner feelings of shame and worthlessness. This may be seen as a way for survivors to run away from the problem and as an attempt to pass themselves off as "normal." One of the results of sexual abuse is emotional confusion. The survivor is overwhelmed by waves of feeling that are out of control. Since survivors do not have the power to directly manage and control these internal feelings, they find some external area of life that can be controlled. This activity often involves organizations or careers that are socially approved. It is usually pursued to the exclusion of some other area of life, like intimate relationships, that are too close to the survivor's uncontrollable feelings. The excessive organization, constant business or workaholic tendencies keep the survivor preoccupied with external things to prevent the memories and internal feelings from emerging. The survivor is afraid to stop the over-compensating activity for fear of being overwhelmed again by the memories and feelings associated with the sexual abuse.

It isn't necessary or desirable for survivors to give up highly successful areas of their lives. Organizational skills, productivity and a career are important skills and valuable assets. The survivor will need to slow down a little and be still long enough for the memories and feelings to emerge. Unfamiliar with both the emotional highs and lows that come when feelings emerge, the survivor needs to slowly alternate between the overcompensating activity and allowing the feelings to emerge. In time the survivor will achieve a balance between activity and feelings that includes recovery from the sexual abuse. A supportive partner will take cues from the survivor's behavior and encourage facing the feelings without taking on too much too fast.

Cleanliness Compulsion

Survivors often feel tainted as a consequence of the sexual abuse and become obsessed with the neatness and cleanliness of their surroundings. The survivor may compulsively straighten the whole house or perhaps only one room such as the kitchen or bedroom. The washing compulsion may include frequent showers or baths as well as continual handwashing or excessive concern with clean clothes and laundry. Cleanliness on the outside may help the survivor feel a little better, but ultimately this is a futile attempt to use an external solution for an internal problem.

Recovery for the survivor means finding a way to deal with the internal shame and feelings of being tainted or damaged goods. Understanding partners can accept the survivor's cleanliness compulsion without ridicule or complaint. Since survivors with a cleanliness compulsion are often easily offended by smells, the partner can make reasonable efforts to avoid being offensive. If the survivor's neatness compulsion is too intrusive on the partner's living space, perhaps both can negotiate a designated part of the house where clutter can be allowed. As the survivor recovers the cleanliness compulsion may be confined to smaller and smaller areas, perhaps down to a single dresser drawer.

Anxiety

Sexual abuse causes fear which shows up as an anxiety that continues to grow stronger until the abuse issues are resolved. This ranges from occasional anxious feelings to an almost constant state of anxiety with severe panic attacks. The state of anxiety may be related to specific phobias or to a more general state of agoraphobia. Common anxieties and fears reported include fear of:

being in crowded places
traveling, accidents, getting lost
collapsing, fainting, getting sick, being paralyzed
entering shops, standing in line
going mad, dying, losing a loved one, harming others
    (especially a child)
loss of confidence, insecurity, loneliness, and depression.

Survivors are often bewildered over their anxious state. They wonder, "What is wrong with me? Why am I feeling like this?" The stress of being unable to find an obvious cause for the anxiety creates an increasing spiral of fear, adrenaline and anxiety. It may show up in panic attacks, severe heart palpitations, dizzy spells or sudden collapse. When survivors feel an anxiety attack coming on, they may abruptly withdraw from a social situation and rush for home. Once home they may remain isolated and afraid to leave for fear of having an attack in a public place.

A lasting cure for anxiety attacks cannot be found until the underlying issues of sexual abuse have been resolved. Sometimes anxiety attacks remain a problem and seem to have a life of their own after the abuse issues have been addressed. In this case desensitization exercises may be needed to treat the anxiety.

Desensitization, according to Dr. Claire Weekes, consists of four steps:

1. Facing the anxiety producing situation
2. Accepting the feelings
3. Floating above the paralyzing fear
4. Waiting for the anxiety to pass

A survivor may need the support of the partner in order to face the anxiety-producing situation. Accepting the feelings means recognizing that some anxiety and fear is a natural response to a stressful situation and doesn't mean anything is wrong. Fighting the fear by tensing up and preparing for flight only increases anxiety. "Float. Don't fight!" is the advice that allows the wave of fear to pass on without catching the survivor in the turbulence of panic. Letting go and waiting for the feelings to pass is the last step. If no resistance is offered, the anxious feelings are fleeting. They quickly spend themselves, allowing the survivor to get on with the job at hand.

Survivors may need a lot of support for the initial desensitization cycle. Partners and friends can supply necessary support until the survivor can manage the four steps independently. Then the survivor can respond to anxiety and fear with the internal advice, "So what — do it anyway."

Depression

Chronic depression is one of the most common complaints reported by survivors of sexual abuse. This is prolonged depression lasting two weeks or more with significant physical symptoms including constant fatigue, unexplained aches, changes in eating or sleeping habits, inability to relax and slowed speech or body motions. Thought patterns are disturbed and confused, showing an inability to concentrate or take interest in anything, often with intrusive thoughts of suicide. The emotions of chronic depression are overwhelming hopelessness, feeling worthless, destructive self-blame, shame, no longer caring and the absence of pleasure.

About half of the depressed survivors complain of physical rather than emotional symptoms. They often complain of headaches, insomnia, anorexia, constipation or chronic fatigue, but say nothing about feeling sad, hopeless or discouraged. Some depressed survivors seem to be unaware of their depression. Chronic pain, weight loss or gain and diminished sexual desire are also classic symptoms. Other common complaints are withdrawal, overactivity, body or muscle aches, feelings of guilt, worthlessness, joylessness, anxiety, lack of energy and low self-esteem.

Self-blame is a depression-prone condition that results when a survivor is accused of causing the sexual abuse. Being treated as the scapegoat makes survivors feel they can never do anything right. As adults, scapegoats become depressed and assume they are responsible for every misfortune whether they are actually at fault or not. Survivors often think of themselves as damaged goods who do not deserve happiness, joy or success in life. Any misfortune that happens simply confirms their negative view of themselves and deepens their spiral of depression.

Survivors obtain relief by seeking out an empathetic person to confide in. Partners can make themselves available for this function. Allowing survivors to put their feelings into words is a healing process that prevents the mental defense of denying the reality of the problem. A nonjudgmental partner can provide an objective response or another perspective. This helps survivors see where their thinking may be going astray and focus on one problem at a time. After several conversations the partner can offer some short-term goals or suggest some steps the survivor can take to recover from the situation. Partners who share experiences that have given them strength and hope may supply survivors with the courage to rise out of depression.

Shame

Having a shame-based identity is an indirect consequence of sexual abuse. Although sometimes conscious, shame is usually denied and repressed, appearing in periodic shame attacks and feelings of unworthiness. Dominating the survivor's whole identity, shame is at the root of many other emotions and influences social behavior and self-concept. For example, shame causes anxiety about being good enough, fear of getting too close and anger if exposed. Low self-esteem is another consequence of an internal shame-based identity.

The devastating effects of sexual abuse produce shame in four ways. Sexual abuse breaks interpersonal bonds, causes trauma or stress, induces personal humiliation and becomes a family secret. A shame-based identity is an almost certain consequence of childhood sexual abuse. Since parents are supposed to be the source of love who only punish or hurt when their children are bad, children who are abused can only conclude they are bad. Making this assumption and believing they are responsible for the abuse is a way to take control over and make sense of an out-of-control family situation.

Sexual abuse at an early age profoundly affects the survivor's ability to trust. The abused child does not have the maturity to see the cause of the sexual abuse as parental lack. The only possible explanation is that there is something wrong with the child, and this is the beginning of a shame-based identity. The survivor's sense of identity derives from the family, and since the sexual abuse is something wrong with the family that cannot be divulged, there must also be some secret internal defect in the survivor. Sexual abuse is almost always deeply traumatic and stressful. The survivor's trauma or stress lingers as unresolved grief and bottled-up emotions, laying the foundation for a shame-based identity. Survivors cannot help but feel personal humiliation as a result of the sexual abuse. This feeling causes the survivor to conclude that some deep personal defect brought on the sexual abuse. This slips into an identity based on shame.

Survivors begin recovering from shame by coming out of denial about the shame associated with the sexual abuse. Survivors need to stop running away from it and accept the shame that drives current behavior. There's no way to solve a problem that can't be acknowledged. The partner can provide an accepting and nonjudgmental setting for the survivor to share the burden of the struggle with shame. By talking about it, the survivor may find that shame begins to lose its hold.

Enjoyed It/Re-initiated It

Sometimes it comes to light that on some level the survivor enjoyed the sensations that accompanied the sexual abuse experience. The survivor may even have initiated repetitions of the experience to have these feelings again. If either of these occurred, it is usually very troubling to the survivor and is one of the most deeply shaming things to admit.

Sex is a natural function. A pleasurable response to certain kinds of stimulation is automatic whether it is desired or not. It is not the survivor's fault if this occurred and it does not excuse the abuse or make it okay. Since touch is a basic human need, the survivor may have taken action that initiated a recurrence of the abuse or made it more likely to recur. This sometimes happens when the survivor had no other source for nurturing touch and didn't receive enough caring and attention.

By talking about the shame and sense of guilt about enjoying or re-initiating the sexual abuse, the survivor comes to understand that the abuser was still responsible. Supportive partners will express compassion and emphasize that the survivor did not deserve to be treated that way or put into the position of asking for attention in that way. This in no way shifts the responsibility away from the abuser. The survivor is not at fault and should not be made to feel blame or guilt.

7

Understanding The Abuser

Why try to understand the abuser? Wouldn't confronting and punishing the abuser do more good?

Understanding how and why the abuser acted is important for the survivor, not the abuser. Survivors need to explore the full extent of their abuse and usually feel the need to understand the underlying causes that led to their abuse. Survivors often need to see how the abuser fits into their lives. Understanding the abuser may be the missing piece that makes sense of the survivor's role in a multi-generational puzzle. Understanding the abuser also allows the survivor to uncover all potential areas of abuse, given the abuser's personality and mode of behavior. This then helps to place the sexual abuse experience in context and enables the survivor to gain a larger perspective that will be useful in later recovery.

Confrontation may or may not be desirable or necessary for the survivor's recovery. The choice of whether to confront the abuser or report the abuser to the authorities is an individual one that can only be made by the survivor. Survivors must make their own choices based on their own circumstances and the likely results and consequences. Understanding the abuser may be helpful for the survivor to make an informed decision.

A more important consideration than getting revenge or punishing the abuser is assisting the survivor in coming to peace with the sexual abuse experience. After the early stages of recovery — including remembering, believing, understanding, grieving and anger — the survivor will be ready to move beyond the "sexual abuse survivor" identification. As part of later recovery, understanding the abuser may help the survivor become relieved of lingering resentment. This may also make forgiveness a possibility.

Ultimately, the goal is for the survivor to gain the self-awareness necessary to make independent choices for the future, choices not colored by the past. Since we are all products of our history and our environment, understanding the abuser's place will help us understand ourselves. Acknowledging what happened and being aware of its potential influence allows us to isolate and counteract its negative effects. Most abusers were themselves abused and failed to accomplish this task. This is our opportunity to look back, clearly see generational patterns, and become the cycle-breakers. Understanding the abuser will assist us in our determination not to pass this burden on to our children.

Responsibility

Part of understanding the abuser is knowing that the abuser was responsible. Survivors did not choose to be sexually abused and are not responsible, no matter what they may have done or failed to do. Even if the survivor was scantily clothed, made enticing remarks or acted suggestively, the abuser was the one who committed the act. Being sexually abused is not an appropriate consequence for the survivor's ignorance or poor judgment. Being raped is not justifiable punishment for poor taste in clothing or style.

The abuser may even have tried to shift the responsibility to the survivor by saying something like, "Look what you made me do." Another attempt to shift the burden onto the survivor might have been, "You are the only one who can help me through this." However, regardless of the circumstances, the abuser had the control or should have had the control to prevent the abuse from occurring.

Fear Of Exposure

On some level, abusers know what they have done is wrong and are afraid of exposure. To coerce their victims into keeping the secret, they insist it will be the victim's fault if anyone finds out. Blame is shifted to the victim for the possible consequences of the abuser's actions: arrest and jail; loss of job, money or house; breakup of marriage or family. Abusers intimidate their victims with escalating threats of no more treats or gifts, physical beatings and even death. To reinforce their threats, abusers are known to have tortured or killed family pets or other small animals in front of the victims of childhood sexual abuse.

Out of false loyalty to their abusers, survivors of childhood sexual abuse often keep the secret long after the abuser has any power to carry out the threats. This may happen on an unconscious level, since for many survivors their memories do not return until after the death of the abuser. In other cases the memories may only return when the abuser has become old and frail. Survivors often feel guilty about breaking the silence or confronting when the abuser is in poor health and is not expected to live long. Survivors need to know that their mental health and recovery may be more important than maintaining a false appearance of family harmony or letting the abuser take the secret to the grave. By the consequences of their own actions earlier in life, elderly abusers have lost the right to be left alone to die in peace.

Abuse Of Power

Sexual abuse is more about the abuse of power and control than it is about the abuse of sex. Abusers are in the position of power and control or place themselves in that position. Having gained the upper hand, the abuser uses sex as a weapon or tool to obtain the rewards of having power over another person.

The abuse may have been disguised as discipline or punishment. The abuser may have distorted beliefs that rationalize the abuse. For example, "I can punish you however I like because I am the parent." A distorted belief system does not make sexual abuse okay. Even if it was handed down from a previous generation, the abuser is responsible for maintaining it and using it improperly as justification for sexual abuse.

The abuser's power may also have been found in superior intellectual ability or emotional control that enabled the abuser to persuade or entice the survivor into acquiescence. Having gained the survivor's submission, the abuser may have tried to share the guilt and responsibility by saying, "We are both in this together and we will both be in trouble if anyone finds out." The abuser may also have tried to shift the illusion of control to the survivor by saying, "You like it when I do this, don't you?" or "If it starts to hurt, just tell me and I'll stop." The fact remains that the survivor was not initially in collusion with the abuser. The abuser was the one in control.

Abusers who commit rape are often motivated by anger and the need to have power over their victims. They typically use far more force than necessary to overpower their victims, inflicting brutal wounds, swearing insults and forcing their victims to commit other degrading acts. The rape is either an expression of revenge and retaliation for nonspecified rejections and hurts or an act of conquest that establishes a sense of power and control. The sexual abuse of rape is clearly in the service of anger and power, with its purpose being the expression of hostility or the humiliation and domination of the victim.

The act of rape is a consequence of the abuser's failure to achieve an adequate sense of identity and self-worth. The abuser does not have the psychological resources to cope with the demands of life and becomes frustrated. Unable to receive approval and discharge conflict through socially acceptable channels, impulse control breaks down. The abuser allows the internal conflicts to be expressed through the act of rape with its associated hostility and imposition of power and control. To the abuser, rape is an assertion of self and an attempt to gain self-esteem through a forcible show of mastery and strength.

The abuse of power also distinguishes sexual abuse from innocent sexual exploration between siblings or playmates. If there is a significant difference in size or maturity or an age difference of four or more years, it was probably sexual abuse. Also if one person was in an actual or perceived position of power and control and used it to make the experience happen, it was probably sexual abuse. This is particularly true if it was accomplished over the survivor's objections. Another indication is that sexual exploration and curiosity is satisfied in a few brief incidents within a short period, while sexual abuse is usually repeated over a longer time.

Dysfunctional Background

Most abusers have come from dysfunctional family backgrounds. This does not excuse their behavior but it may place the problem in perspective. Coming from alcoholic, incestuous or otherwise dysfunctional families, abusers are likely to have grown up with unmet emotional needs. Lacking the maturity to get their needs met in healthy adult relationships, abusers turn to children or other victims who can be overpowered.

Dysfunctional families fail to teach the use of functional boundaries, and most abusers have little knowledge of or respect for the boundaries of others. For example, abusers might not be aware that exposing children to the sight and sound of adult sexuality is abusive. Abusers tend to behave in aggressive ways, intruding physically and emotionally into the boundaries of their victims, and they do not seem to be aware that they are being offensive. In playing with children an abuser is likely to be a little too rough or push tickling and touching a little too far. "What's the matter? I was just kidding or just playing," is an excuse frequently used by abusers.

Narcissistic

Abusers often have narcissistic personalities and are incapable of empathy with others. Being totally caught up with themselves, they believe they are sharing themselves when using their victims for their own gratification. They are grateful to their victims for the services received, but they are completely unable to see the damage caused by their actions.

A survivor overpowered by a narcissistic abuser may continue to submit in order to receive the abuser's gratitude, which is mistaken for love. Alternatively, survivors may lose their own identities and adopt the pleasure experienced by the abuser as their own. Survivors who have been the victims of narcissistic abusers tend to have under-developed personalities and to over-identify with the accomplishments of others in their lives. They may become parents who are over-identified with their children, another group at risk of becoming abusers.

Over-Identified

Over-identified abusers cannot see clearly the distinction between themselves and their victims. Often themselves victims of narcissistic abusers, they feel fulfillment through others. They experience vicarious pleasure in the inappropriate sexual fondling or caressing of their children. They see the sexual abuse as a gift of love rather than the imposition of their sexuality onto an unwilling victim. They feel pleasure only in the pleasure they can give rather than finding any pleasure of their own. They manipulate their victims through guilt, saying, "How could you do that to me?" when their victims try to escape.

Survivors of over-identified abusers have difficulty individuating and creating a life of their own. Since the sexual abuse may not have been brutal or overt, the survivors may have difficulty realizing that they are victims of sexual abuse. They often remain unmarried and overly attached until the death of the abuser. It may be late in life before such survivors begin to have an identity of their own and to acknowledge that the attachment was abuse, not love.

Misdirected Love

One of the lies abusers use to justify their actions is to describe the abuse as a way of expressing love. The abuse may have been described as "spanking" rather than the assault and battery that it was. Would it still have been described as loving behavior if it were done to another adult? Whether the justification is rationalizing or a true belief, the result is still sexual abuse. The abuser's statement, "This is the way I show you I love you" does not change fondling, stimulation or invasion from sexual abuse into love.

Sexual abuse of the misdirected love variety also masquerades under the guise of personal hygiene or parental instruction. Sexual abuse may occur in the bathroom with the explanation, "This is the way I wash you" or "This is the way I take care of you." Sexual abuse passed off as instruction may be described as seeing how the survivor will handle it or providing necessary experience for future situations.

Adults unable to experience intimacy in their adult relationships may turn to children to fulfill their intimacy needs. They may believe it is expressing love to bring their children into their intimate conversations. The blurring of generational boundaries causes the survivors of such abuse to have difficulty distinguishing healthy expressions of love from inappropriate and emotionally abusive confiding of personal matters. It is incestuous and emotionally abusive to treat a girl as a "little mother," "little wife," or date for an adult male and to treat a boy as a "little man" or an escort for an adult woman.

Re-enactment

Many abusers were survivors from a previous generation's sexual abuse. Survivors are at risk of becoming abusers and passing the abuse on to the next generation.

The possibility of a survivor becoming an abuser is a difficult issue to face since most survivors have such strong negative feelings toward abusers. However, it is an important one. Survivors who have not recovered a full sense of self and what it means to be loved themselves will pass on a defective view of love to their children. Since survivors often have an unclear perception of boundaries, their parenting styles may abusively violate the boundaries of their children.

Understanding abusers, how they are like us and how they are different from us, is the best way to avoid having re-enactment become a reality. Acknowledging and dealing with our negative thoughts is healthier than letting them emerge unconsciously and against our will. We do honor to our complete personalities when our self-examination includes our shadow selves as well as our public persona. Looking at our dark side with the support of a recovery program enables us to keep it in check and be cycle-breakers.

8

Getting And
Staying Healthy

Having assumed responsibility for our own recovery and taken the steps necessary to start resolving our own core issues, we now need to turn our attention toward the goal of living a healthy life in recovery. As our issues are resolved, there is a gradual shift in focus away from the painful and difficult core issue work and toward the happiness and joy of living and staying healthy. Recovery is the process of getting and staying healthy for the rest of our lives.

Since many of us have come from dysfunctional backgrounds, we may not have a clear image of healthy behavior. Even if we had models of healthy behavior at one time, in our current circumstances as partners of sexual abuse survivors, it is easy to backslide into dysfunction. This description of healthy ongoing behavioral characteristics is what constitutes recovery.

In the process of living a healthier life, we must remember that we are each responsible for only one life, our own. Others are responsible for their own lives which they must live in their own individual ways. It's not healthy for us to try to exert undue influence or control over another's life. Getting healthy and staying healthy ourselves is the best we can do. As partners of sexual abuse survivors, the most helpful thing we can do for the survivor's recovery is to be healthy and functional ourselves.

It's good for us to remember it is by looking within that we find our true self, the undamaged inner child. In the discovery of the child within, we recover all the wonder, truth, goodness and beauty that make us who we are. In doing so, we find within ourselves a wellspring of love and power that can sustain us throughout life.

By continuing to pursue a path of inner healing, we will discover our true selves and radiate a sense of health. We will truly know and believe that we matter, that we are worthy of love and deserve happiness. We will grow into a strong sense of identity, facing life boldly and giving ourselves approval. In our interactions with others we will establish clear and flexible boundaries. We will stand up for ourselves, loving ourselves and initiating action to satisfy our own wants and needs.

In intimacy we will show our tender feelings; with strength we will put forth our powerful feelings. In our love relationships and friendships we will attract and be attracted to strong and healthy personalities. For mutual support we will maintain a network of friends to call on for help when we are in need. We are on a path of lifelong learning and personal growth that knows no limits.

A P P E N D I X

Starting A Partners' Support Group

Although there are not many, there may already be a partners' support group in your area. Ask at survivors support groups and mental health organizations to find out what is available. If you have looked for help and have been unable to find it, you may want to consider starting a partners' support group.

Starting a support group requires an initial organizational effort followed by the commitment to maintain its momentum until it can become self-sustaining. It takes work but is not an impossible task.

In the process of finding out whether there is already a support group in your area, you may have come into contact with others who have the same need. Ask them to help in the organizational effort and share the work.

Find a location for your support group meetings, preferably a public place. Consider mental health facilities, churches and other locations used by AA or other 12-Step programs. Once you have found a location, the structure of the support group can be established.

As part of the organizational effort or at the initial meeting, a decision must be reached concerning the format for the meetings. Will the group follow the format of 12-Step meetings like Alcoholics Anonymous and Adult Children of Alcoholics? Will the meeting use the 12 Steps and 12 Traditions? Will meeting space rental and incidental expenses be paid from the donations of the participants? Will each person be allowed to share without comment or will the meeting allow cross-talk — conversational exchanges and confrontation?

Create a flyer explaining the purpose of the support group and announcing the date, time and location of the first meeting. Set the first meeting date far enough in advance for people to respond. If the flyer is laid out on standard letter size paper, it can easily be copied and distributed. Distribute the flyers through survivor support group meetings or other support group meetings that allow announcements of interest. Post them at mental health facilities and churches.

Use the attached meeting format and partners' support group purpose statements or adapt them to meet your needs. Add the reading of the 12 Steps and 12 Traditions if your group decides to use them.

PSA Meeting Format

This is the regular meeting of the Partners of Sexual Abuse Survivors Anonymous support group. The meeting lasts from 8:00 to 9:30.

A PSA support group is a fellowship of men and women who meet to share our experiences of living with a survivor of sexual abuse, our common problems and the solutions we have found.

Read the "Welcome Statement."

Have someone read "The 12 Steps."

Have someone read "The 12 Traditions."

Have someone read "Why Does It Affect Me?"

Have someone read the "Map To Recovery."

Ask each person to introduce themselves.

Collect contributions.

Introduce the chairperson and/or select topic.

Read the "Closing Statement" at the end of the meeting.

Welcome Statement

We welcome you to the Partners of Sexual Abuse Survivors Anonymous support group and hope you will find in this group the help and friendship we have been privileged to enjoy.

We who live with a survivor of sexual abuse understand as perhaps few others can. We too were lonely and frustrated. However, in this support group, we discover that no situation is really hopeless. We can find contentment and happiness.

We urge you to join us. Even though it is not easy, sharing our experience has helped many of us to find solutions that lead to serenity. So much depends upon our own attitude. As we share our common problems, we find that they lose their power to dominate our thoughts, our feelings and our lives. The loving interchange of help among members makes us ready to receive the priceless gift of serenity.

This support group is an anonymous fellowship. Everything that is said here, in the group meeting and member to member, must be held in complete confidence. Only in this way can we feel free to say what is in our minds and hearts, for this is how we recover ourselves and help one another.

The 12 Steps

1. We admi .ed we were powerless over the effects of incest, rape or sexual abuse in any form, that our lives had become unmanageable.
2. Came to believe that a Power greater than ourselves could restore us to sanity.
3. Made a decision to turn our will and our lives over to the care of God as we understood God.
4. Made a searching and fearless moral inventory of ourselves.
5. Admitted to God, to ourselves, and to another human being the exact nature of our wrongs.
6. Were entirely ready to have God remove all these defects of character.
7. Humbly asked God to remove our shortcomings.
8. Made a list of all persons we had harmed and became willing to make amends to them all.
9. Made direct amends to such people whenever possible except when to do so would injure them or others.
10. Continued to take personal inventory and when we were wrong promptly admitted it.
11. Sought through prayer and meditation to improve our conscious contact with God as we understood God, praying only for knowledge of God's will for us and the power to carry that out.
12. Having had a spiritual awakening as a result of these steps, we tried to carry this message to others, and to practice these principles in all our affairs.

The 12 Traditions

1. Our common welfare should come first; personal progress for the greatest number depends upon unity.
2. For our group purpose there is but one authority — a loving God as God may be expressed in our group conscience. Our leaders are but trusted servants; they do not govern.
3. Partners of sexual abuse survivors, when gathered together for mutual aid, may call themselves a PSA group, provided that as a group, they have no other affiliation. The only requirement for membership is association with a survivor of sexual abuse.
4. Each group should be autonomous, except in matters affecting another PSA group or another anonymous 12-Step program.
5. Each PSA group has but one purpose: to help partners of sexual abuse survivors. We do this by practicing the 12 Steps to recovery ourselves, by encouraging and understanding the sexual abuse survivor, and by welcoming and giving comfort to other partners of sexual abuse survivors.
6. Our PSA group ought never endorse, finance or lend our name to any outside enterprise, lest problems of money, property and prestige divert us from our primary spiritual aim. Although a separate entity, we should always cooperate with other anonymous 12-Step programs.
7. Every group ought to be fully self-supporting, declining outside contributions.
8. PSA 12-Step work should remain forever non-professional, but our service centers may employ special workers.
9. Our groups, as such, ought never be organized; but we may create service boards or committees directly responsible to those they serve.
10. PSA groups have no opinion on outside issues; hence, our name ought never be drawn into public controversy.

11. Our public relations policy is based on attraction rather than promotion; we need always maintain personal anonymity at the level of press, radio, TV and films. We need guard with special care the anonymity of all members of all anonymous 12-Step programs.
12. Anonymity is the spiritual foundation of all our traditions, ever reminding us to place principles above personalities.

Why Does It Affect Me?

If you are the partner of a sexual abuse survivor, you are not alone. Recent studies show that by the age of 18, one woman in three and one man in four has been sexually molested. It has been estimated that these statistics are low due to under-reporting, especially for male victims. We also know these statistics are based on a definition of sexual molestation that includes only the most flagrant and overt kinds of sexual abuse.

Self-declared sexual abuse survivors also include those who were forced to hear or see others abused, exposed to pornography, involved in voyeurism or exhibitionism, verbally abused and raped or abused as adults. Including these in the definition of sexual abuse significantly increases the number of survivors and partners of survivors.

As the issue of the survivor's sexual abuse begins to emerge, many of us as the partners of sexual abuse survivors wonder why we are so strongly affected. We may not fully understand what happened and its effects, or we may not be able to accept it as reality. We may react to being told of the abuse with disbelief, feelings of guilt or a strange kind of curiosity. Although we didn't know for sure, some of us may have suspected abuse from the survivor's reactions to being touched in a certain way.

Many partners of sexual abuse survivors feel hurt or cheated by the experience and feel like blaming the abuser for causing it or the survivor for not preventing it. Some of us feel overwhelmed because we have had repeated relationships with sexual abuse survivors. In spite of our best efforts, many of us find that our relationship is deteriorating and our sex life is not fulfilling or satisfying.

We may feel angry and full of rage and not know how to deal with it. We may be confused by guilty or shameful feelings due to society's negative attitude toward sexual abuse. Although our private feelings are natural and understandable, at some level we know it would not be helpful to express them to the survivor. We do not know where else to turn.

Since sexual abuse happens to survivors of either sex and regardless of sexual preference, we may be in heterosexual, gay or lesbian relationships. Regardless of these apparent differences, we share a commonality of experience and feelings. Whether the abuse was heterosexual or homosexual, incest, rape, occurred in childhood or adulthood, was long ago or recent, we belong here. In this group all of us can find comfort and understanding.

Map To Recovery

We start the road to recovery by taking responsibility for ourselves and keeping the focus on our own core issues.

We must first resolve any primary dependencies such as drug addiction or alcoholism and then control any secondary dependencies such as compulsive eating, spending or working that might interfere with facing our feelings. As partners of sexual abuse survivors, we learn to deal with issues of co-dependency that are bound to arise. These may include such core issues as boundary deficiency, detachment, over-control, people-pleasing and caretaking. By educating ourselves on the issues faced by sexual abuse survivors, we find we are able to be supportive without taking on the survivor's problems.

We choose to be healthy and to live happy and functional lives ourselves, since we know that is the best thing we can do for both our own and the survivor's recovery. In taking care of ourselves, we come to believe in our value and special qualities and to generate from within a healthy sense of self-esteem.

Accepting the reality of our physical, mental, emotional and spiritual aspects, we obtain a clear concept of ourselves and are able to be fully present in our own identities. In all interactions, we practice using healthy boundaries that protect us from being offended and offensive. We are particularly careful to establish healthy boundaries with our survivors, since many have become accustomed to boundary violation and are uncomfortable with functional boundaries. We also face the possibility that we ourselves are sexual abuse survivors.

As competent adults, we are able to express our wants and take action to meet our own needs. With wisdom and maturity, we find we are able to do this without placing undue burdens or demands on our survivor and without being hurtful. In this way we model healthy and functional behavior.

In relationship with our survivor we share our thoughts, feelings and inspirations, nurturing a mutual sense of intimacy and connectedness. We invite our survivor to do the same and respectfully support our survivor's increasing self-esteem, developing identity and personal reality.

Since no one or two individuals have the depth of resources to overcome the issue of sexual abuse alone, we reach out to others for support. We trust that friends will be able to keep our confidences, and we risk asking for the help we need. We find that in interdependency we are able to assume our rightful place in a mutually supportive network of friends. We work the Steps, stay active in support groups and take part in continuing personal growth activities. We strive to increase our overall wellness and to improve our balance in all significant areas of our lives.

Closing Statement

In closing, the opinions expressed here were strictly those of the person who gave them. Take what you like and leave the rest.

The things you heard were spoken in confidence and should be treated as confidential. Keep them within the walls of this room and the confines of your mind.

Will all who care to join me in the Lord's Prayer or the closing meditation.

Closing Meditation

I put my hand in yours, and together we can do what we could never do alone.

No longer is there a sense of hopelessness, no longer must we each depend upon our own unsteady willpower.

We are all together now, reaching out our hands for power and strength greater than our own, and as we join hands we find love and understanding beyond our wildest dreams.

BIBLIOGRAPHY

For Partners

Bass, Ellen and Davis, Laura. **The Courage to Heal: A Guide for Women Survivors of Child Sexual Abuse**, Part Four: For Supporters of Survivors. New York: Harper & Row, 1988.

Kritsberg, Wayne. **Healing Together.** Deerfield Beach, Florida: Health Communications, 1990.

Maltz, Wendy and Holman, Beverly. **Incest and Sexuality: A Guide to Understanding and Healing**, Chapter 10: Survivors and Partners Working Together. Lexington, Massachusetts: Lexington Books, 1987.

McEnvoy, Alan and Brookings, Jeff. **If She Is Raped: A Book for Husbands, Fathers, and Male Friends.** Holmes Beach, Florida: Learning Publications, 1984.

For Survivors

Bass, Ellen and Davis, Laura. **The Courage to Heal: A Guide for Women Survivors of Child Sexual Abuse.** New York: Harper & Row, 1988.

Butler, Sandra. **Conspiracy of Silence: The Trauma of Incest.** San Francisco: Volcano Press, 1985.

Finkelhor, David. **Sexually Victimized Children.** New York: Free Press, 1979.

Forward, Susan and Buck, Craig. **Betrayal of Innocence: Incest and Its Devastation.** New York: Penguin Books, 1979.

Gil, Eliana. **Outgrowing the Pain: A Book For and About Adults Abused as Children.** Walnut Creek, California: Launch Press, 1984.

Maltz, Wendy and Holman, Beverly. **Incest and Sexuality: A Guide to Understanding and Healing.** Lexington, Massachusetts: Lexington Books, 1987.

Sisk, Sheila and Hoffman, Charlotte. **Inside Scars: Incest Recovery As Told by a Survivor and Her Therapist.** Gainesville, Florida: Pandora Press, 1987.

Utain, Marsha and Oliver, Barbara. **Scream Louder: Through Hell And Healing With An Incest Survivor And Her Therapist.** Deerfield Beach, Florida: Health Communications, 1989.

Williams, Mary Jane. **Healing Hidden Memories: Recovery For Adult Survivors Of Childhood Abuse.** Deerfield Beach, Florida: Health Communications, 1991.

Anonymous 12-Step Recovery Programs

There are Anonymous 12-Step recovery programs for almost any core issue. Most of them are patterned after Alcoholics Anonymous (AA) and use some variation of the original 12 Steps of Alcoholics Anonymous. The meeting formats are also based on the AA meeting format.

Most recovery programs are open to anyone who wants to attend and welcome the participation of newcomers. Everyone is invited to listen and learn. No one is asked to say anything except to introduce themselves by their first name. Those who speak, talk about their own experiences without criticizing others. Anonymous recovery programs stress confidentiality and request that nothing be repeated outside of the meeting about who attended or what was said.

The established Anonymous 12-Step programs can be found by calling the information number listed in the telephone book. The newer programs can be located by calling the local county mental health agency or information and referral service. The Anonymous 12-Step programs listed below are available in most areas.

Adult Children of Alcoholics (ACA/ACoA)
P.O. Box 3216
2522 W. Sepulveda Blvd. #200
Torrance, CA 90505
(213) 534-1815

Alcoholics Anonymous (AA)
P.O. Box 459
Grand Central Station
New York, NY 10163-0459

Al-Anon
Family Group Headquarters
P.O. Box 862
Mid Town Station
New York, NY 10018-0862

Co-dependents Anonymous (CODA)
P.O. Box 5508
Glendale, AZ 85312-5508
(602) 944-0141

Incest Survivors Anonymous (ISA)
P.O. Box 5613
Long Beach, CA 90508-0613
(213) 428-5599

Narcotics Anonymous (NA)
16155 Wyandotte St.
Van Nuys, CA 91406
(818) 780-3951

Overeaters Anonymous (OA)
4025 Spencer St. #203
Torrance, CA 90503
(213) 542-8363

Sex and Love Addicts Anonymous (SLAA)
P.O. Box 88
New Town Branch
Boston, MA 02258

Survivors of Incest Anonymous (SIA)
P.O. Box 21817
Baltimore, MD 21222
(301) 282-3400